# WHEN YOU NEED A SPECIAL SERMON SERIES

D0109953

Publishing House
St. Louis

Copyright © 1981
Concordia Publishing House
3558 South Jefferson Avenue
St. Louis, Missouri 63118

Manufactured in the U.S.A.

1   2   3   4   5   6   7   8   9   10   WP   90   89   88   87   86   85   84   83   82   81

Library of Congress Cataloging in Publication Data
Main entry under title:

When you need a special sermon series.

    By Paul L. Maier and others.
      1. Lutheran Church—Sermons.  2. Sermons, American.
I. Maier, Paul L.
BX8066.A1W52          252′.04133         81-476
ISBN 0-570-03836-7                      AACR1

# PREFACE

As desirable as it is to preach on the texts of the lectionary lessons with their virtues of unity and variety, now and then a special series of sermons can be used to good effect. If you are asked to serve (or supervise) a vacancy, or if you are in charge of a retreat or camp service, or if you just want to deal with a certain subject in more depth—here is a sermon series that provides you with thought starters, coordinated themes, and developed subjects.

From eight authors come six such mini-series of three sermons each, on various topics, timely and timeless. They are ready for use in case of emergency—or just in case you are looking for a fresh series of contemporary sermons.

And, to make your task of preparation easier, each sermon provides parallel Scripture readings and appropriate hymn suggestions.

May your use or adaptation of these sermons bring the power and refreshment of the Gospel to your hearers.

—The Publisher

# CONTENTS

# GOD IN HISTORY

## God in History—Greece

ACTS 18:1

Christians often have the mistaken notion that God has revealed Himself *only* in the Bible, and that all the evidence for His existence, majesty, and will are restricted to its pages. Now Scripture *is,* indeed, God's fullest revelation of Himself in words, just as Jesus Christ is His ultimate revelation in person. And yet our God, in His mercy, uses many other channels to reach us with the Good News that He creates, preserves, saves, and sustains us.

Besides the Bible, God, for example, also uses nature to reveal Himself. The wonders of His creation are especially apparent in these delightful summer months, when we emerge from the cocoons of winter to celebrate the green grandeur of earth or the vastness of a star-studded universe. This "natural knowledge of God" can be very convincing, as St. Paul himself observes: "Ever since the creation of the world His [God's] invisible nature, namely, His eternal power and deity, has been clearly perceived in the things that have been made" (Rom. 1:20). For that reason, he also announced to the pagans at Lystra during his First Missionary Journey that God "did not leave Himself without witness, for He did good and gave you from heaven rains and fruitful seasons, satisfying your hearts with food and gladness" (Acts 14:17). Nature herself, then, sings out a perennial paean of praise to God as Creator and Preserver.

So, too, does history. God has scattered proofs of His activity throughout the past. Why do you suppose God's favorite name for Himself in the Old Testament was "the God of your fathers, the God of Abraham and Isaac and Jacob"? He was showing the people of Israel that they had a God who acted in history in their behalf and was marvelously faithful in delivering them from Egypt, preserving them in the desert, and maintaining them in the Promised Land. God further acted in history when He decided that the time had fully come to send mankind His ultimate revelation in the form of a Child at the Nativity, and for this reason Luke (2:1) sets the whole Christmas story into its historical and political context with his famous

7

passage: "In those days a decree went out from Caesar Augustus...." Was it strange to begin the Christmas story with a pagan emperor? Not strange at all! God was sending Jesus, not into some spiritual never-neverland or Divine Disneyland, but into Judaea: a specific province of the historical Roman Empire.

This sermon series will try to show how God has revealed Himself not only in religious history—the Bible—but *also in secular history.* To accomplish this, we will focus on three great metropolises of the ancient world as stages for God's intersection with history: Corinth in Greece, Ephesus in Asia Minor, and Rome in Italy. Christianity's greatest missionary—St. Paul—visited all three (in that order) during his journeys for the Gospel, and he spent more time at these places than anywhere outside his hometown. Clearly, they were of prime importance in Paul's ministry, as they are prime examples of how God has used also history— Biblical and secular—to reveal Himself and accomplish His purposes.

## I. The Biblical Record

The setting is Paul's Second Missionary Journey. He and his associates had set foot in Europe for the first time, encountering both blessing and opposition in the Greek towns of Philippi, Thessalonica, and Athens. Paul delivered his memorable address on Mars Hill at Athens, cultural capital of the ancient world, but he did not stay there. Instead, as our text records, "After this, Paul left Athens and went to Corinth." Indeed, the apostle spent the next 18 months in the Greek metropolis on the isthmus, his longest, most important sojourn to date.

The rest of Acts reports Paul's exciting ministry at Corinth. If you don't recall its fascinating detail, why not use this chapter for your family devotions this evening? You will read how Paul first announced the Good News in the Jewish synagog at Corinth, converting no less than the ruler of the congregation. Quite naturally, the others urged Paul to preach elsewhere, and—with charming subtlety—he did so: right next door to the synagog, at the home of a Christian convert!

Over the next year and a half, the apostle's ministry was so powerful that many became Christians, including a gentleman named Erastus, who was no less than the city treasurer of Corinth (Rom. 16:23). Such success worried the remaining members of the synagog, and they indicted Paul before Gallio, the Roman governor of Greece. Christians often fail to realize how *very* important this trial was for the future of the faith. In fact, it was the first test case for Christianity since Jesus stood before Pontius Pilate. If Paul lost this one—and God had not made other arrangements—

the birth of Christianity in the Mediterranean world could have been aborted. Happily, however, Gallio dismissed the charges. He told the prosecutors that if this had been a criminal case he would have judged it. "But since it is a matter of questions about words and names and your own law . . . I refuse to be a judge of these things"(Acts 18:15). So he threw the case out of court.

Paul had triumphed. He was now free to continue preaching in Greece, Asia Minor, Judaea, and Rome. The faith would not only survive but thrive. And Corinth became so important in Paul's ministry that he would visit the city again on his Third Missionary Journey and write several important letters there which are epistles in the New Testament.

A happy ending to quite a drama. But is it true? Did it really happen? It may be a Bible story, but is it really *history?*

## II. Secular History

God "did not leave Himself without witness, . . . " also in records from the ancient world which are quite *outside the New Testament.* Our merciful Lord—knowing the doubting sorts we are—has provided not one but *two* separate channels in which to communicate the story of how the Gospel was planted in Corinth. The best and fullest, of course, is Luke's inspired version in Acts 18. But God has acted also in *secular* history to support His Biblical version.

Ancient history and archaeology—far from being dangers to the faith—are in fact Christianity's best friends. See how this works out in the case of Corinth. From history we learn *why,* in the words of our text, Paul favored Corinth over Athens for his missionary activities. Athens, by this time, was a "has-been" in terms of political power in Greece. The Roman "proconsul of Achaia" (translate that as "governor of Greece") now ruled the province instead from the city of Corinth. Here, at the center of power, Paul would preach the faith.

Archaeology—first cousin to ancient history—provides several stunning discoveries which categorically support the account in Acts. The very place where Paul first preached at Corinth can be identified along the Lechaion Road—the main north-south artery of the ancient city—because a marble block was uncovered here with the inscription, "The Synagogue of the Hebrews." The *macellum* or meat market Paul refers to in 1 Cor. 10:25 was located across the street. The very *bema* or tribunal where he stood before the Roman governor Gallio has been unearthed, and its marble slabs stand in a fine state of preservation at the southeastern corner of the main square in the ruins of Corinth.

Critics once voiced their doubts that so high a Corinthian official as the city treasurer should have become a Christian, as Paul implies at the close of his letter to Rome. Likely Erastus and his title were simply fictitious, they argued. But archaeology has brought to light a limestone plaza near the city theater in Corinth with the following notice inscribed at the corner in large, bronze Latin letters, translated: "ERASTUS, DURING HIS CITY-TREASURERSHIP, LAID THIS PAVEMENT AT HIS OWN EXPENSE."

And what about Gallio, Paul's judge who dismissed the charges against him? Both archaeology and history combine to give us important additional information on the man. An inscription discovered at Delphi both names "Lucius Junius Gallio" as "proconsul of Achaia," and dates his year in office as A.D. 51-52, providing an anchor date for Pauline chronology. Gallio himself may have only a "bit part" in the New Testament, but he played a major role in the history of the early Roman Empire. He was brother to the famous Stoic philosopher Seneca and uncle of the poet Lucan. Fifteen years later, he would be involved in a conspiracy against the emperor Nero and be forced to commit suicide.

When Luke, then, peopled his history of the early Christian church, he did not use imaginary figures or cardboard characters. All of the personalities in the drama at Corinth were authentic, genuine, real. This is not story, but history.

### III. Lessons from History

Other correlations between Biblical and secular history could be cited, but the point is this: Corinth was a definite place—and A.D. 51—52 was a definite time—in which God intersected with history by sending His greatest missionary to bring the Gospel to Greece. He wisely chose the political power center of Greece as his base of operations, at which no less than Rome's governor himself gave the faith freedom of expression. It was a dramatic milestone in the spread of Christianity, and, for all the drama, this was far more than play-acting: it *actually happened.* Secular history and archaeology fully support all principal elements in the New Testament account.

If you doubt or have friends who disbelieve this segment of God's revelation, then you—or they—are not simply denying Scripture, but are quite foolishly ignoring all the other supporting hints God has provided from history to support the New Testament. If "the fool has said in his heart, 'There is no god' "(Ps. 14:1), it must take a *double* fool to reject both Scripture and history too!

Thank God, however, it usually works the other way. This dual evidence time and again has rather overcome doubt and reinforced faith. Dozens of examples could be given of how skeptics examined the relevant evidence from history and archaeology, matched it with Scripture, and were convinced and converted. The message of how God sent Jesus into the world to atone for our sins by His innocent suffering and death, and how He made us righteous in His sight despite our own unworthiness in the greatest of all triumphs—that over death itself in the resurrection—was of such paramount importance that He permitted history and archaeology to add their testimony to the truth of His gospel.

The places and events of history say something important about God's plan of salvation to us even today and in our particular place. God comes into our cities, towns, and streets just as He once lived and died among us in the person of His only Son, Jesus Christ. He made the journey to our planet and to the cross out of love for a world that was doomed and dying. In the Savior He redeemed this very world we occupy. He sought the lost in the corners and crannies of the world the way a woman looks for a missing coin or a shepherd for a lost sheep. And then, paying the penalty for sin and defeating death, He established His church, planted it on this planet, made it His holy body, and turned it loose in history to reclaim the lost and dying in each succeeding century. As the ascended Christ He governs and rules the events of history for the benefit of His people, all who have the brand of Baptism, all who are under His sway and will witness the ultimate victory of their Lord.

If God has used history in the past to accomplish His will, then we can also be certain that He continues to do so in the present and will do so in the future. What an enormous comfort this is for believers: to realize that events finally happen—not in response to the juggernaut of chance, but in accordance with His higher plans for us and for the world. With this assurance, we can face the future with supreme confidence, knowing that the Gospel, the church, and all true Christians are ultimately in His divine hands.

God *has* truly revealed Himself in a marvelous variety of ways. Praise Him for His flexibility and mercy in giving us alternative channels by which to appreciate His grace. May we never show folly in rejecting His multiple approach to us in Christ, in Scripture, in the sacraments, in nature, and in history.

## Parallel Scripture Reading

Acts 18

**Suggested Hymns**

O God, Thou Faithful God
Our God, Our Help in Ages Past

# GOD IN HISTORY

## God in History—Asia

ACTS 19:26

One of the most attractive of St. Paul's many positive personality traits was his courage. He enjoyed being at the cutting edge of Christianity, never preaching the Good News in secure or receptive areas, but always deep in "enemy territory" among the pagans of Greece, Asia Minor, and Rome. This may help to explain his strange concentration on the city of Ephesus in Asia Minor, where he stayed the longest—three years—of any of his preaching stations. Ephesus was the most unlikely beachhead for Christianity in the entire Mediterranean basin. Paul must have calculated that if he would conquer for Christ here, then the Gospel could be victorious everywhere, particularly in the land which is today called Turkey. This, in fact, is what happened, and it constitutes another powerful example of God's intervention in history, of how events in the ancient past seemed to move according to divine design for the spread of the Christian message.

### I. The Biblical Record

Paul had trained his sights on the city of Ephesus very early in his ministry. In fact, he was aiming for this metropolis during his Second Missionary Journey when God interrupted his plans. He was "forbidden by the Holy Spirit to speak the word in Asia"(Acts 16:6), and Asia, here, means the Roman province of western Asia Minor. Many Christians are troubled by this passage, but they need not be, for it was all a matter of higher scheduling. First the Gospel was to be preached in Macedonia and Greece, and then, with far more time at Paul's disposal, he would indeed reach all of Asia with the Good News through his long ministry at Ephesus.

Like Corinth, Ephesus was a wealthy commercial center, but it also sheltered the most bizarre collection of pagan priests, exorcists, temple prostitutes, magicians, cultists, and charlatans in the entire Roman

Empire. Since the great marble Temple of Artemis was the pride of the city and one of the fabled Seven Wonders of the Ancient World, Ephesus annually played host to hordes of pagan pilgrims from all over the East during the festival of Artemis each spring.

Why should Paul have wished to plant the seed of faith in so hostile a ground? Because he saw it all as a supreme opportunity for Christianity. By counteracting the baleful influence of all this wild religious potpourri, he could sublimate its fanaticism instead into enthusiasm for Christ, he resolved. And since Ephesus was the principal city in the whole eastern Aegean world, all Asia would learn of the faith if it succeeded here.

The Biblical record in Acts 19 provides the fascinating detail, demonstrating how much of Paul's strategy succeeded in fact. As was his habit everywhere else, Paul began by preaching in the synagog, and for three months he testified boldly that Jesus was the promised Messiah of the Old Testament. Again, as elsewhere, opposition arose, and the apostle had to transfer his preaching station. Fortunately, he was able to use the "hall of Tyrannus," apparently a Greek teacher or philosopher who owned the hall and rented it to Paul for a nominal fee. Some ancient New Testament manuscripts add that Paul taught here "from the fifth hour to the tenth" each day, that is, from 11 a.m. until 4 p.m., the hottest part of the day when Professor Tyrannus and his students had left the classroom. In any case, for two years Jews and Gentiles, Asiatics and Greeks could enroll in the "University of Saint Paul" to hear the Christian message, and this platform proved an extraordinary funnel for the faith in Asia Minor.

Since both God's Word and the wonders He accomplished through Paul were widely reported in the city, many Ephesians who believed now gave an extraordinary response. They gathered together in a great heap their books on magic, obscene materials, idols, figurines, statuettes, and parareligious paraphernalia, and set fire to them. The Book of Acts even reports that the value of this bonfire was 50,000 pieces of silver—probably about $20,000.

Quite an impact the Holy Spirit had made through Paul with the Gospel! That impact, evidently, also had an economic edge, because one great, vested interest at Ephesus was outraged: the idol-manufacturing industry. The guild of the silversmiths felt threatened. Probably it was the president of the guild, a fellow named Demetrius, who called his fraternity together and wailed that Paul's preaching against their product was about to put them out of business. In the words of our text, "And you see and hear that not only at Ephesus but almost throughout all Asia this Paul has persuaded and turned away a considerable company of people, saying that gods made with hands are not gods."(Could anyone have delivered a more pithy line against idolatry?)

A howling must have gone up from the silversmiths, but it was not enough to lead to a general riot. So Demetrius cleverly widened his alarmist tactics by including no less than the number one tourist attraction in all of Asia Minor: the great Temple of Artemis at Ephesus. "And there is danger," he added, "not only that this trade of ours may come into disrepute but also that the great goddess Artemis may count for nothing, and that she may even be deposed from her magnificence, she whom all Asia and the world worship" (Acts 19:27).

This had the desired effect. The problems of one guild affected the general public no more than a strike in one industry does today; but undermine the number one tourist attraction of Ephesus, and the whole city would suffer. Now it became a general cause, and much of Ephesus ran to the civic assembly point: the great theater. For almost two hours and from all the galleries, a great, rhythmic chant welled up: "GREAT IS ARTEMIS OF THE EPHESIANS! GREAT IS DIANA OF THE EPHESIANS!" Two of Paul's traveling companions, Macedonian Greeks named Gaius and Aristarchus, were targets of this demonstration, and they had to hear the awful chant for endless minutes, in mortal danger of their very lives from mob action. Typically, St. Paul wanted to go on stage at the theater to try to calm the crowd, but he was detained by the Christians of Ephesus, who realized that it could have meant his death.

Rather, the situation was saved by civil authority. The town clerk of Ephesus rushed onto the stage, held up his hands for quiet, and proceeded to win control of the riot by using good crowd psychology. Concurring with them about "Great Artemis," he boldly cleared Paul's friends of any charges of impiety and declared that the whole matter should be aired in a civil suit, if necessary. Any further rioting would only lead to a swift crackdown by the Roman authorities, he warned.

That was the end of the disturbance. But it was not the end of Christianity at Ephesus, only its strong beginning. The church which Paul planted thrived and grew, becoming the mission base for converting much of Asia Minor. Later, Paul would write one of his most important epistles to the Christians here, and it was to this city that the disciple John seems to have brought Mary, the mother of Jesus, and where he wrote his own epistles. Later on, one of the great ecumenical councils would meet in Ephesus as a totally Christian city.

Here, then, is another success story of the early church, another intervention of God in history. *But did it really happen?*

## II. Secular History

As in the case of Corinth, our Lord has provided several strategic "back-up systems" in history and archaeology for His activity and the course of the Gospel. The city of Ephesus was just as important in secular history as it was in religious, one of the greatest metropolises of Greek antiquity. The great Temple of Artemis was indeed one of the "Seven Wonders" luring pilgrims from all over the Mediterranean, and the ruins of this prestigious shrine are now clearly exposed, because the swamp which had flooded them has finally been drained, and one of the temple columns has been re-erected.

The figure of Artemis herself—more a fertility goddess than the Roman equivalent moon goddess Diana—has been found in many of the excavations here, and in all sizes ranging from figurines (probably the very stock in trade of Demetrius and his ilk) to full-size marble statues. The Artemis motif surfaces everywhere in the classical ruins, mute testimony to the accuracy of Luke's account and the monomania of a people who could shout for two hours in her behalf!

But more. The very theater into which the people rushed and where they raised this chronic clamor has been fully excavated. Scraped into the side of a hill overlooking the ruins of Ephesus, this sprawling theater is one of the largest of the ancient world, boasting a capacity of 24,000 seats. Spectacular even in ruins, the great theater is an acoustic marvel, and Luke's hint that "the whole city" was involved in this uproar but could quiet down to hear the voice of one city clerk is easily demonstrable today: a person on center stage can be heard at the topmost rows without even raising his voice. And sitting in the vast tiers of seats as they face westward toward the harbor of Ephesus, one can almost hear the faint echoes of a strange cry, "Great is Artemis of the Ephesians!"

But this is quickly drowned out by the more triumphant shouts of a victorious Christianity: "For by grace you have been saved through faith! . . . There is one Lord, one faith, one baptism, one God and Father of us all, who is above all and through all and in all. . . . Put on the whole armor of God!. . . Stand therefore! . . . And take the helmet of salvation, and the sword of the Spirit, which is the word of God!"—all phrases from Paul's great letter to the people of *this* particular city. What a contrast from the chant about the vaunted greatness of a goddess no one ever saw—except in ugly idols, the egg-studded, hundred-breasted statues of Artemis now sheltered in the Ephesus museum, or in wothless silver figurines still peddled in the tourist shops. Truly, "gods made with hands are not gods."

### III. Lessons from History

Small wonder, then, that Paul could launch his heroic phrases of encouragement Ephesus-ward. What a message he had! Great is *God*—not Artemis—because the sovereign Creator who made a perfect world did not let the sin of mankind fracture His work but repaired it all in Jesus Christ, the God-become-man, who perfectly fulfilled the divine law but took upon Himself the consequences of our failure to do so. His innocent suffering and death became our redemption and our life, so that whoever believed in Christ—Greek, Ephesian, or American—might be saved.

In the short-range view at Ephesus, Paul might have felt that he had failed; that, after three years of preaching and teaching in town, God had withheld His blessing on his efforts. The raucous praise to Artemis from thousands of hoarse throats was no great commentary on the growth of Christianity in that city! And yet, the apostle had lit all the human fuses at Ephesus which, under God, would lead to the conversion of the whole city in time.

Today, similarly, we too often take the short rather than the long-range view of God's activity in history. What seems failure to us at the moment may actually be success in the divine, supremely wide-angled panorama on which God paints. Like Paul, we must not be discouraged if our current efforts or affairs seem to reflect no higher design or dimension. We are probably focusing on a tiny colored-stone rather than stepping back to see the sweep and glory of the whole mosaic.

Paul could truly *believe* what he preached because he had found God breaking into history for him on the Damascus Road, and he had interviewed those who had spent three years and more with Jesus during His earthly ministry. In turn, he passed the evidence on to us. At Ephesus, he and Luke left behind all the geographial, archaeological, and historical correlations we need to anchor this account to hard fact and firm belief.

On Palm Sunday, Jesus had told the Pharisees who rebuked the multitudes praising Him, "I tell you, if these were silent, the very stones would cry out"(Luke 19:40)! In another sense, the very stones *do* indeed cry out—the artifacts, the ruins, the hard evidence from archaeology. How pathetic that some weak-kneed Christians are afraid of historical and archaeological investigation in the Holy Land and elsewhere because "someday they might discover something that will disprove the Bible" or "undermine our faith." Quite the opposite is the case!

And so "put on the *whole* armor of God!" One way is to show the world how very *credible* is our incredible faith! "You shall love the Lord your God with all your heart, and soul, *and mind,"* Jesus told us (Matt. 22:37). With this sort of evidence He touches our minds, too, demonstrating that while Christianity may involve a "leap of faith," that leap is not made into theologically thin air or with the blindfold of ignorance. The glory of our faith is that its record of God intervening in history through His apostles is convincingly true. Corinth showed that. So does Ephesus, and so do many other Biblical sites.

### Parallel Scripture Reading

Acts 19

### Suggested Hymns

The Church's One Foundation
Oh, for a Faith That Will Not Shrink

# GOD IN HISTORY

## God in History—Italy

ACTS 28:14

With one exception, the great religions of the world today were founded in the uncharted mists of the past, or by luminaries about whom, quite frankly, *very* little accurate information is known. Hinduism, for example, offers no names, no founders, no history, or biography at its roots. Buddhists, on the other hand, point with pride to Gautama Buddha as founder, but traditions about his life were not recorded until two and a half centuries after his death and are therefore unreliable. The site of the sacred Bo Tree under which he sat to conceive Buddhism has never been located.

In China, Confucius and Lao-Tzu—traditional founders of Confucianism and Taoism, respectively—are enigmatic personalities about whom little is known. In Japan, Shinto has no founder, no sacred Scriptures or even dogma, while elsewhere in Asia, Zoroastrianism derives from Zarathustra, another prophet whose life cannot even be dated to the nearest century!

In utter contrast to these nebulous, hazy, beclouded origins, Christianity burst on the world not in legend but in fact, not in traditions but in history, not in some never-neverland but in Palestine. God provided His ultimate revelation in the form of a man—Jesus of Nazareth—about whom *much* is known, who interacted with other eyewitnesses, some of whom reported their experiences in virtually the same generation, and in locatable places which can easily be identified today.

We have visited two of these sites in this series: Corinth and Ephesus. Today we follow St. Paul to his final destination, the imperial capital of the Mediterranean world, the city of Rome.

## I. The Biblical Record

The apostle had long determined to visit the hub of the Empire. "I have often intended to come to you," he wrote the Christians at Rome (Rom. 1:13), but it took nothing less than a direct appeal to Caesar himself against a local miscarriage of justice to bring him there. And the trip—made at government expense—was not without its dangers: a horrendous storm-tossed voyage from Crete to shipwreck on the island of Malta, which, incidentally, is told in some of the most accurate maritime reportage in ancient literary sources. Luke mastered his facts well, whether writing of events on land or sea.

The final chapter in Acts traces in detail the last legs of Paul's journey from Malta to Syracuse, Rhegium, and Puteoli. No imaginary sites, these: today, Syracuse is a metropolis in southeastern Sicily and spelled exactly the same way, while Rhegium is Reggio, on the tip of the Italian boot, and Puteoli is now Pozzuoli on the Bay of Naples, the harbor where Paul's ship docked. Even the little villages on the highway up to Rome—Forum of Appius and Three Taverns—not only have been identified, but demonstrate that Paul, Luke, and their entourage were using the famous Appian Way to travel to Rome.

"And so we came to Rome," Luke reports in our text, thus giving a final destination and focus to his great early church history—the stirring account of how the faith was seeded across the Mediterranean according to Jesus' own formula: "You shall be my witnesses in Jerusalem . . . Judaea, and Samaria, and to the end of the earth" (Acts 1:8)—here, specifically, Asia Minor, Greece, and Italy.

Just as surprising as this geographical precision was the warm reception accorded Paul and Luke in Italy. Already at Puteoli, the Christians in the port city begged the apostle to stay a week with them, while believers in Rome dispatched a welcoming delegation to the 33rd and 43rd milestone on the Appian Way in order to extend their enthusiastic welcome.

For the next two years, Paul, even though he was in detention, would build on this reception to preach a truly eternal Gospel in the heart of the "Eternal City." His success, even in chains, was astonishing, for he could write to the church at Philippi (1:12-13): "I want you to know, brethren, that what has happened to me has really served to advance the Gospel, so that it has become known throughout the whole Praetorian Guard and to all the rest that my imprisonment is for Christ." Evidently, there was even a group of Christians worshiping in Nero's palace itself, for Paul closed his letter: "All the saints greet you, especially those of Caesar's household." (Phil. 4:22)

But was Paul perhaps inflating his claims, as some critics have charged? Or was Luke, who reported 3,000 converts at the first Christian Pentecost, exaggerating his numbers there, as well as the success of Paul's preaching in Rome? Is the evangelist not very likely presenting a "glory story" here rather than sober history, an idealized version of how the church leap-frogged across the Mediterranean to announce its message in Rome? Some skeptics have dismissed much of the Acts account as an early Christian adventure story or even novel—a bundle of triumphalist traditions, in essence, and nothing more.

## II. Secular History

God, however, "has not left Himself without witness . . . " also in secular history. All the extra-Biblical "back-up systems" fairly shout the fact that Luke is accurate and Paul's claims are *not* inflated. One of the most stunning correlations between Scripture and ancient history occurs at this point. Even though Luke breaks off his Acts account with the famous "unresolved fade-out" in chapter 28, his account is resumed, not by a Christian author, but by Cornelius Tacitus, a *pagan* Roman author who had no brief whatever for Christianity and would have been the last person in the world to inflate any statistics on them.

Nevertheless, in his famous passage at *Annals* xv, 44, Tacitus tells how the Roman people blamed Nero for the great fire of Rome in A.D. 64, but that the emperor deflected the blame by blaming others as arsonists— incredibly, the Christians of Rome:

> To suppress the rumor [that he had set fire to Rome], Nero fabricated as culprits, and punished with the most refined cruelties a notoriously depraved class of people whom the crowd called "Christians." The originator of the name, Christus, had been executed in the reign of Tiberius by the governor of Judaea, Pontius Pilatus. . . . First, the self-acknowledged members of the sect were arrested. Then, on their information, a vast multitude was condemned. . . .

The last phrase—a *vast multitude*—is startling, because how could there have been so great a number of Christians available for persecution only 31 years after Pentecost in a Rome which was 1,500 miles away from Palestine *unless* the movement had the kind of powerful ignition described by Luke in Acts, as well as the success of Paul's preaching in Rome claimed in Philippians? For a philosophy or teaching to spread this far, this fast, in the ancient world is absolutely unparalleled, and Tacitus' reference to the "vast multitude" does not even include those larger numbers of Christians who went underground to keep the faith alive.

This first horrifying persecution of this many Christians occurred only four or five years after Luke writes of Paul's Roman reception, and only *two* years after Paul's claims that even the Praetorian Guard— Rome's government police—had heard the Gospel. And so—just like the stones—history cries out the truth of the Scriptural account. Any fair-minded ancient historian would have to conclude: Luke wrote with accuracy and care. Paul's claims were *not* inflated. The Gospel had achieved a startling result, even statistically, in ancient Rome.

### III. Lessons from History

The past, then, cries out indeed. And well it should, because history, by its very chronological division into years B.C. and A.D., "before Christ" and "in the year of our Lord," proves, in essence, to be not just history but *His*-story, the ripple effect in humanity of what happened when God decided to save what He had created by sending His Son into the world to suffer, die, and rise again in our behalf, that whoever should believe *His-story* (another spelling for the Gospel) should be saved. The whole past, then, pivots about a Jesus Christ who was crucified for our transgressions, but raised again for our justification.

Because the core message was this important, God chose his Biblical writers well. St. Luke, the author of the three texts in this series, deemed it appropriate that he write his Gospel, since he had "followed all things accurately" so that his readers might "know the truth" (Luke 1:3-4). This is the same goal of any honest historian, and, indeed, the very term "history" derives from the Greek *historia* which means "inquiry"—precisely Luke's activity in preparing his version of the Good News.

Martin Luther once called music the handmaiden of theology. The great reformer was right, of course, but he might have included several other handmaidens too. Nature, history, and archaeology would easily qualify as well. All of them are extra props to buttress the faith, supplementary witnesses to the truth of the Gospel, resonances and echoes of apostolic preaching, and very convincing "fall-out" from the original explosion of Christianity. In His infinite versatility, God the Holy Spirit uses Word and Sacrament preeminently, but also some of these auxiliary channels to strengthen our faith.

What God did, He does, and will do. He used history in the past, He is using it now, and He will continue to govern its course. In our turbulent times and in an era of continuing crises like the present, this truth will sustain us amid all adversity. Sacrifices may be necessary. Like St. Paul, we may have to give up security, comforts, standards of living, or even life itself, but the crown of eternal life toward which we press is God's own goal for us all in Christ. This gives final meaning to our very existence, strength for the trying days ahead, the full assurance of final victory.

God *was* in history, *is* in history, *will be* in history.

### Parallel Scripture Reading

Acts 28

### Suggested Hymns

Built on the Rock the Church Doth Stand
For All the Saints Who from Their Labors Rest


# GOD IN NATURE

## Birds, Butterflies, and God

PSALM 139


Occasionally life seems to lose direction and purpose. People carry on with no spring in their step and no song in their heart. They seem doomed to the mood of Macbeth: "Tomorrow and tomorrow creeps in this petty pace from day to day, to the last syllable of recorded time; and all our yesterdays have lighted fools the way to dusty death." Caught in such a dismal view of the days they might make their theme verse, "If that's all there is, let's break out the booze and have a ball—and keep on dancing."

Is life like a squirrel cage where you go round and round and get nowhere fast? Do our days add up to nothingness? Is life in the final analysis a dead-end street? Many people think so. Therefore they look upon life as simply a game of craps.

### Luck—Fatalism—Humanism

As he caresses his rabbit's foot or some other charm he utters, "That was a lucky break." Every piece of good fortune is attributed to chance. When good appears, such a person merely thanks his lucky stars. If peril crosses his path with adversity, it will be chalked up as a streak of bad luck.

Others will simply ride the boat of life, never really manning the oars or using the rudder, for whatever will be will be. Fatalism is the flag under which they sail. Everything is determined by fate, and there is little you can do about it. Islam pronounced such predestination. Allah is whimsical, and the winds of fate may blow you around with no predictability. People who ascribe to this philosophy use expressions such as: "The cards of life are stacked"; "When my number is up, my number is up." The soldier in conflict may talk about the "bullet with his name on it." Somtimes Christians are duped into this insidious rationale when they attribute everything that happens in life as "the will of God." Thus God gets blamed for tragedies that man brings on himself with his own stupidity and sin.

Then there is that group of confident people who usurp God's place with their exalted concept of self. It is humanism that makes man the center of the universe. Man takes a bow for any accomplishment and achievement that dots the landscape of history. This haughtiness is held aloft in William Henley's poem, "Invictus." The last verse proclaims:

> It matters not how straight the gate,
> How charged with punishments the scroll,
> I am the master of my fate;
> I am the captain of my soul.

In contrast to these pronouncements comes the fact of divine providence. Creation is not a spontaneous chemical reaction to nothingness, nor a joke of chance. A Creator stands within and without His creation, sustaining and directing it. This universe is God's controlled experiment, and we are more than the product of a population explosion. God does not take his eyes off us. Nothing will go unnoticed, and no rose is "born to blush unseen." The psalmist declares, "O Lord, Thou hast searched me and known me! Thou knowest when I sit down and when I rise up; thou discernest my thoughts from afar" (Ps. 139:1-2). Then he exclaims in astonishment and awe, "Such knowledge is too wonderful for me; it is high, I cannot attain it" (Ps. 139:6).

As we scan the pages of the Sacred Writings, we find statements such as these: "He leads me . . . " (Ps. 23:2-3). "I will instruct you and teach you in the way you should go" (Ps. 32:8). "Trust in the Lord with all your heart, and do not rely on your own insight. In all your ways acknowledge Him, and He will make straight your paths" (Prov. 3:5-6). "My times are in Thy hand" (Ps. 31:15).

When Paul spoke to the people at Lystra he told them, "[God] did not leave Himself without witness, for He did good and gave you from heaven rains and fruitful seasons, satisfying your hearts with food and gladness" (Acts 14:17). Perhaps we should take another look into His creative works around us to remind us how His sustaining and guiding hand is still operative in the lives of even the creatures.

### The Marvelous Monarch

When the days of Indian summer invade the State of Minnesota, the monarch butterfly gets ready for a southern journey. It is a beautiful creature painted with regal orange and black. This butterfly, which weighs about as much as a paperclip, brightens our gardens and summer fields. But in the fall there is a mass exit from the land that will soon be wrapped in snow and ice.

Where does the butterfly go? It was a puzzle for many years. At last, however, Dr. Fred Urquhart, zoologist at the University of Toronto, solved the mystery. These Minnesota monarchs were found in numbers ranging in the tens of millions wintering in a 20-acre grove of pines in the Sierra Madre Mountains of Mexico. There, during the winter months, the conditions are perfect for the monarch's needs to survive and perpetuate its species.

By the month of March, as the temperatures climb, these monarchs mate and soon fly off to Texas where the milkweed is ripe and full grown. The females lay their eggs—the caterpillar emerges three to twelve days following; it feeds on the milkweed—the chrysalis is formed; and in two weeks the adult butterfly emerges. From egg to adult takes about five weeks.

The parents die en route north. The offspring arrive in Minnesota in late May or early June. Of course, at the time there is the ripening of the milkweed! This generation mates and then lives out its brief lifespan of approximately six weeks. Their offspring are born in late August or early September.

Now comes an unbelievable twist of nature. The Mexican monarch's great grandchildren that are born in Minnesota in late summer have a chemical or hormone change which gives them a life expectancy of over seven months in comparison to the six weeks of the other generations. This enables them to make the long 2,000-mile flight to the wintering sites in

Mexico and live there till spring. Imagine that distance being completed by such a small insect with frail wings, buffeted by winds, drenched by rains!

How do the monarchs navigate? The butterflies that make the trip south are at least three generations removed from those who made the flight the prior year. How can they possibly find that 20-acre plot in the Mexican mountains? There is an awesome void in our knowledge of this mystery. I guess only the Creator understands. So far the secret has been locked within the tiny brain of this gorgeous little creature.


### The Migratory Birds

Another mysterious form of providence in nature is that of the migratory birds. The oldest known observation on bird migration ever put down in writing is that of the prophet, "Even the stork in the heavens knows her times; and the turtledove, swallow, and crane keep the time of their coming" (Jer. 8:7). Each spring and fall nature lovers are enthralled by the miraculous movements in the sky as the birds respond to their inner urge to move to a different climate. Many reasons are pondered as to the promptings of migration. Food supply and nesting conditions play a part in their flight across pathless skies. Many wonderings as to their flight patterns and their navigational skills leave our curiosity only half answered.

The wood ducks, for example, have their birthplaces imprinted indelibly on their memory. In their annual migration to Minnesota, wood ducks fly to the same place—often the same tree—in which they were born. One of the most remarkable flights is that of the tiny rufous hummingbird that measures under four inches, yet flies over 4,000 miles—Alaska to Mexico.

People of Bible times did not know the far reaches to which the migrating birds journeyed, but they were aware of the directions. Job records the hawk stretching its wings to the south, and Is. 18:1 speaks of "the land of whirring wings which is beyond the rivers of Ethiopia."

We again pause to wonder. Inside the mind of each bird must be a complicated system of triggers and timers that function as a computer. Now a computer must always be programmed by a master hand. For the birds, we must admit, that hand is the hand of God.

On an autumn evening when the Canadian geese are drifting through the sky we hear their high-pitched honking, alternating clear and then faint, carried by the breeze. The sight and sound quicken the pulse. One is conscious of not possessing wings. Our imagination accompanies their flight, and we wonder what wilderness they came from and where they will find refuge. The whole scene stirs our soul to restlessness.

Will God guide us also through the days and years that sometimes seems like a trackless maze? Robert Browning thought so:

> I see my way as birds their trackless way,
> I shall arrive! What time, what circuit first,
> I ask not: but unless God send His hail
> Or blinding fireballs, sleet or stifling snow,
> In some time, His good time, I shall arrive:
> He guides me and the bird. In His good time.

This awareness happened to a young man once at the sunset of a day among the Massachusetts hills. He was lonely and fearful of the future. He had just left home to find work in his chosen profession. Suddenly against the crimson sky he saw a lonely bird, winging its solitary way southward. He watched until the bird disappeared. But the magic of the moment lingered. For William Cullen Bryant it became a guidepost. If an unseen Power could guide a lonely bird, it would most certainly lead him also. He wrote the following lines in a poem, "To a Waterfowl:"

> He, who, from zone to zone,
> Guides through the boundless sky thy certain flight,
> In the long way that I must tread alone
> Will lead my steps aright.

### A Plan for a Man

Perhaps the story of Joseph reveals to us concrete evidence as to God's care and involvement in a person's life. Joseph's father had a whole raft of sons. However, Joseph occupied a special spot in his father's heart. He got a coat of many colors. What a lucky kid!

But his brothers hated him. They resented the favored treatment which Joseph seemed to receive. Jealousy and hatred welled up within them. One day while out tending the flocks, they threw the young Joseph into a dry well. On second thought, they changed their mind about leaving Joseph there and instead they sold him to a caravan heading for Egypt. They told their father that some wild beasts had attacked and killed Joseph. What an unlucky boy he was!

While in Egypt, Joseph was sold into slavery. He was a bright boy and rose to high levels of achievement and responsibility in the home of the rich merchant who owned him. Luck began to shine on Joseph again. But it was short-lived. The boss's wife wanted to have an affair with this young, virile lad. Joseph refused to play around with her. As a result the lady of the house felt rejected, and she struck out at Joseph. She maligned and slandered Joseph's name and reputation. Joseph became unlucky once more.

He sat in jail until one day he was given an opportunity to interpret Pharoah's dream. From that point on he rose to power and prominence in Egypt. Egypt was able to survive a terrible famine and to help neighboring countries. Joseph was second in command of one of the greatest civilizations of the world. How lucky the man was!

There came a day when Joseph's brothers came to Egypt to get grain, for they were facing starvation. Joseph recognized them. Eventually he said to them, "I am your brother." They were scared to death. They knew that he could eliminate them very easily. And he had good reason to do it for they had treated him so badly. After he talked to them for a while, he did not attribute his situation to luck.

We could paraphrase his words to his brothers in this way: "Look, you sold me into slavery. You meant it for evil; but God had a way of using that act to put me here ahead of you to save your lives and that of many people." That is how Joseph viewed his life from the pit in Israel to the second chariot in Egypt.

The God of the butterfly, of the birds, and of Joseph is the God whom we have come to know, love, and trust because of Jesus Christ. It was in the giving of His Son to death on the cross for His helpless and rebellious creatures that God demonstrated the depth and vastness of His love and concern for everyone. That was how God so loved the world. His Father's heart cares not only that we make it through this life safely, fed and clothed, but that we arrive happily—because of His Son and His Son's sacrifice—in the heart of His family and in that place filled with supernatural wonders no eye has yet seen nor ear yet heard. Assured of such limitless love, we can draw the conclusion of St. Paul: "He who did not spare His own Son but gave Him up for us all, will He not also give us all things with Him?"

Joseph knew what we all have to know, that no matter what else happens, this always has been, and always will be, our Father's world. We can blunder and bluster, and yet when a life is handed over to God, He will take the blocks and build His purposes through us. To the person who puts his or her hand in the hand of God, God has promised to uphold and guide. Joseph knew it. Paul knew it. I know it. For the Christian it isn't good luck or bad luck or fate that brought us to where we are today. It is God working in us and through us. It is simply providential!

Following the resurrection, Jesus appeared many times to the disciples and others. Part of it was a testimony to the fact that He had truly risen from the dead. But I also believe that He was attempting to convince them of His continual presence. With doors locked Jesus dramatically dropped in on the disciples. Jesus is not locked up in books, boxes, or church buildings. He made the promise, "Lo, I am with you always, to the close of the age" (Matt. 28:20b).

Jesus is out on the road with His people. He is sitting with them at meal. Jesus laughs and cries with them. Jesus is here. Now! And "the sheep hear His voice and He calls them by name and leads them out"(John 10:3). This awareness of His providential presence transforms life. Henry Ward Beecher, colonial preacher, said, "Time went on, and next came the disclosure of a Christ ever present with me—a Christ that was never far from me, but was always near me as a Companion and Friend, to uphold and sustain me. This was the last and best revelation of God's spirit to my soul."

### Parallel Scripture Reading

Genesis 45:1-15

### Suggested Hymns

Guide Me, O Thou Great Jehovah
Lead On, O King Eternal
O Master, Let Me Walk with Thee
Take My Life and Let It Be


# GOD IN NATURE

## Erosion of Soil and Soul

ROMANS 1:16-32


As one travels across the prairies and the plains and over the majestic mountains of America, the observing eye sees a destructive force at work. It is called erosion. Erosion is the continuous wearing down and sculpturing of the earth's surface by natural agencies such as wind and water. In the past, glaciers have played an important role in the transporting of masses of rock and earth to new locations.

Small rivulets in a farmer's field may cause gullies, and these wash precious soil into streams and rivers. The Mississippi River collects much

sediment throughout its long course, and it deposits 730 million tons of silt
every year into the Gulf of Mexico. John F. Timmons, agricultural
scientist, warns that soil erosion and the accompanying water quality
problems may replace petroleum as the nation's most critical natural
resource problem. For individuals and peoples, loss of topsoil means loss
of wealth, and sometimes loss of the means of subsistence.

Erosion takes place gradually. On a day-to-day basis it seems
relatively harmless. But if you add up the cumulative effect of the centuries,
its toll is deadly. Careless agriculture and lumbering can partially or wholly
destroy the protective canopy and greatly speed up soil erosion on certain
kinds of soil. Unwise cultivation and overgrazing can change a grassland
into a desert.

### Moral and Spiritual Erosion

The moral landscape is also being attacked by a form of erosion. It is
called sin. It binds, blinds, and destroys the good life. It erodes the precious
soil of the soul and leaves in its wake a path of spiritual barrenness. The
little rivulets of sin grow into rushing waters of destruction.

In our text for today St. Paul vividly describes the devastating erosion
of morality that takes place when God is abandoned and people live only to
satisfy their lusts and impulses. The end result is hellishly horrible to
contemplate.

In some cases, Scripture tells us, God will give people over to their
drives and degeneracy—and their lot is hopeless as they separate
themselves from their only possible cure or rescue.

But for those who see the dangers and want to be saved from them, He
provides a new birth and a new nature. "If anyone be in Christ, he is a new
creature; the old things are passed away. Behold, everything is new!" This
is the whole purpose behind the plan of salvation God has made for the
world. "God so loved the world, that He gave His only-begotten Son, that
whoever believes in Him should not perish, but have everlasting life."

In this new relationship we nevertheless go on living in the eroding
world around us and are constantly susceptible to the same forces. It is
important for us to know what to watch for and how to live victoriously in
the face of these strong threats to society, to nature, and to the people of
God.

Some years ago, a city water company circulated information about
the high cost of neglecting to check household leaks in the plumbing
system. In order to portray the facts graphically, a tiny circle only one
thirty-second of an inch in diameter was printed. Opposite the circle

appeared the information that through even so small a hole 6,550 gallons of water would escape in a month's time. Another circle, one-sixteenth of an inch in diameter, the customer was told, would permit 26,230 gallons of water to escape if undiscovered for a month. Finally, opposite a circle one fourth of an inch in diameter was placed the information that through such a hole 375,150 gallons would be lost in a period of one month. That kind of loss costs good money!

Small leaks can cause great losses. There is also tremendous personal power lost through small faults that are commonly looked upon as trivial. Evil is evil in whatever degree it is found. "Little" sins never remain that way. They always grow in savageness. A person who allows himself to tell an occasional lie will wake up some day to find a reputation for being dishonest. An individual who tries drugs for a "kick" will usually find the dosages being increased, and he will be victimized by the habit. The person who misappropriates even small sums of money is on the road to becoming an embezzler of larger amounts. There are no such things as harmless little sins. You cannot have a little nest of gossip, envy, indifference, or selfishness without having them hatch into dinosaurs of destruction. No health authority would tolerate "just a few" typhoid bacilli in a well that supplies drinking water. Neither should we harbor within our personalities a few disease germs of evil. The writer of Hebrews exhorts us, "Let us lay aside every weight and sin which clings so closely . . . " (Heb. 12:1).

The late Dag Hammarskjold put it this way: "You cannot play with the animal in you without becoming wholly animal, play with falsehood without forfeiting your right to truth, play with cruelty without losing your sensitivity of mind. He who wants to keep his garden tidy doesn't reserve a plot for weeds." How do we handle an environmental washout? Maybe observance of the ways by which we cope with erosion in nature will help us find parallel ways of dealing with erosion in the soul.

## Recognize It

If the soil on your land is either washing or blowing away, the first step is to recognize that it is happening. You must realize that the problem will not disappear unless you take steps to stop it. Often it seems easier to miss seeing erosion in your own backyard rather than in the neighbor's plot. A farmer must periodically tour his land and check for signs of erosion.

The same holds true in our lives. Paul says, "Let a man examine himself . . . " (1 Cor. 11:28a). James tells us that we should take a good look at ourselves and see if we are doing the Gospel, "For if anyone is a hearer of the word and not a doer, he is like a man who observes his natural face in a mirror; for he observes himself and goes away and at once forgets what he was like" (James 1:23-24).

Some years ago, during a diphtheria epidemic in a small town, the local doctor took painful precautions to keep the disease from spreading. In his tireless concern for the townspeople he went from house to house examining the throat of every occupant. Still the disease continued to rage. Later it was discovered that the good doctor was the carrier. He forgot to examine his own throat.

When my children were small, I saw a good example as to how we see erosion in the lives of others and not in ourselves. As we prayed before meals, we attempted to have our children fold their hands and close their eyes. This one morning at breakfast our little girl, Debbie, exclaimed right after grace was said, "Daddy, Barak did not close his eyes." I then asked Debbie, "How did you know that Barak didn't close his eyes?" Sheepishly she realized that when she accused her brother she was pointing at herself.

In checking erosion we must survey the landscape of our lives through the binoculars of the Bible. We must stand in the illuminating Light of the Word in order to see the little rivulets of ruination that may be running through our lives.

### Build Dams

Men have built dams since the early days of recorded history. Perhaps the first ones were used to divert the flow of mountain streams into irrigation channels. Today they are also used for creating reservoirs for water supply, for the generation of electrical power, for increasing the depths of streams to make them navigable. And in many areas dams are now being built for flood control. Dams will thus serve to stop, impede, or direct the flow of water.

Dams become a means of stopping the turbulent, uncontrolled waters from sweeping across the land and carrying away the precious soil. The water is good, however, when it is controlled. We all have come into this world with a powerful set of impulses or instincts. These desires were not created nor manufactured by us. They were placed in us by God who made us in His image. The late, great preacher, J. Wallace Hamilton, calls these impulses, "the wild horses we have to deal with." If they are untamed, they will run rampant and cause harm. If they are dammed up and channeled into proper pursuits, they will become great allies in the building of a good life.

Jesus never did want to break the spirit of man, to take the fight out of him and leave him a dried-up cabbage. He wants to take these instincts within us and cause them to be a driving force for service. Luther Burbank believed that every weed is a potential flower. The very qualities that make it a weed could make it a flower. Great sinners and great saints contain much of the same stuff. Paul and Napoleon both had ambition. The difference was that Paul used it in the service of God for the glory of Christ. Napoleon used it to build up his own importance. I think Jesus loved the lust for life that Peter possessed. It caused him to sometimes act impulsively and spontaneously. But there was a magnetism there. And when Peter rose up to preach at Pentecost, there was a liveliness to it all. Bishop Arthur Moore said, "I would rather restrain a fanatic than try to resurrect a corpse."

James and John jostled for positions of high level. They were reaching for the top. Jesus didn't put down their "drive." He redirected it with the statement, "Rather let the greatest among you become as the youngest and the leader as one who serves" (Luke 22:26).

Anger can be self-destructive. But a Christian needs to be able to get mad at injustice and indifference. Abraham Lincoln said about the slave trade, when he saw it with his own eyes as a young man in New Orleans, "If I ever get a chance to hit that thing, I'm going to hit it hard." Martin Luther said, "When I am angry, I preach well and pray better." Yes, anger can be redeemed and redirected as an impulse which we might call creative strife.

By building dams of restraint, God can take our human emotions, stormy though they be, and convert them to constructive and spiritual use. Then they will cease to be causes of erosion.

### Contour Plow

If a farmer has land which is very hilly, he cannot afford to plow and plant his fields by going straight up and down the hills. It would certainly be easier to do it that way, and it would take less time; but when the heavy rains come, much of the crop and soil would just wash down the hill. Therefore, contour plowing is necessary to preserve the land. It is the procedure of following the contour lines of the field. You trace the shape or the slope of the land with ridges and furrows in order to retard erosion. This process is certainly more difficult than merely farming your fields in a straight line. Without it, though, the fields would flush away when floodlike rains fall upon the land.

There is also no easy way for the cultivation of the soul soil. We must learn the arduous task of contour plowing. Jesus said, "If any man would come after Me, let him deny himself and take up his cross and follow Me" (Matt. 16:24). He frankly said the Christian life is for the fighter and not the shirker. At times we may wish we could invite Christ alone for a cozy tea party where we could sit around in comfort and ease. But when Christ comes, He always brings His cross, and the crowd is close behind. Chesterton once said, "Christianity has not been tried and found wanting; it has been found hard and not tried."

A small boy was looking at a geography book. He exclaimed to his mother, "Why is it, Mom, that all the rivers are crooked?" She replied, "I guess it is because the rivers follow the path of least resistance." It is true. Rivers skirt the rocks and boulders and find their way along the unresisting sand. Lives are often crooked for the same reason. It is easier to tell a little lie than to stand firm with the truth. It is easier to be silent in the face of evil than to speak out against it. It is easier to criticize and tear down than to compliment and build up.

Because of the erosional forces of sin we must be willing to fight if we would win. The Christian knows that he will grow only through facing the obstacles and difficulties. Struggle puts color in the cheeks and puts conviction in the cranium. When we stop trying to put the great music of the Gospel in an easier key, we will be far better off.

### Plant Trees

As you drive through the flat plain states of our country, you will notice that some areas have planted long belt-lines of trees and shrubs. They were planted for the purpose of curbing the effects of the winds which would scrape off the thin topsoil and send it sailing in the sky to other regions. These windrows of vegetation also provided shelter for wildlife.

In mountainous country, trees are planted to keep the soil from washing down steep banks. The root system of the trees and shrubs will hold the precious soil in place.

This planting system tells me something about my Christian life. The business of planting trees should occupy more of my time than hunting for weeds. The Quakers had a slogan, "It is better to light a candle than curse the darkness." That is good advice. It seems easier to get people to march in a crusade against something than to get them to stand up for something.

Today demands deeds of love and concern from the people of God. Principles enunciated and hopes expressed are not enough. The best way to fight evil is with positive affirmative action and not with negative haranguings. In this game of Christian strategy the best defense is a good offense. Or we would phrase it in the words of an older pastor whom I had for confirmation instruction: "The best way to fight Satan is to serve the Lord." When you fill your mind with good things, there will be little opportunity for bad thoughts to creep in and get an audience. That is why

Paul exhorts us: "Finally, brethren, whatever is true, whatever is honorable, whatever is just, whatever is pure, whatever is lovely, whatever is gracious, if there is any excellence, if there is anything worthy of praise, think about these things" (Phil. 4:8).

If your lawn is filled with crab grass or some other obnoxious vegetation, you could get down on your hands and knees and spend a lifetime trying to root it all out. Or you could prepare the soil, plant good seed, fertilize it, and allow the good grass to crowd out the bad. Life will work that way, too. Paul tells us, "Do not be overcome by evil, but overcome evil with good" (Rom. 12:21).

Erosion can be stopped in the fields and in life. Follow the four steps: Recognize it; build dams; contour plow; plant trees. Now you can bloom where you are planted and bring forth fruit to the glory of His name! Jesus desires this for you. He does not want to see your God-given potential erode away. His timeless pledge shall always be, "I came that they may have life, and have it abundantly" (John 10:10).

### Parallel Scripture Reading

Galatians 5:13—6:10

### Suggested Hymns

Fight the Good Fight
Jesus Calls Us
Lord Speak to Me
Lord, Keep Us Steadfast in Thy Word

# GOD IN NATURE

## Autumnal Splendor

PSALM 65

The gentle breezes of spring call for nature to bring forth new life. The renewing rains splash on the earth, and the thunder seems to growl out the command—"Grow!" Nature moves slowly as the budding trees are still tightfurled. But then the yellow-skirted daffodil dances shyly on the stage and beckons the rest of the forest and meadow to wake from the winter's nap. The mountains yawn and stretch, and the birds begin their chorus in many harmonious parts. Soon life begins to burst in frenzied activity, and the land laughs with joy as springtime is born.

Nature then seems to settle down for the task at hand. It is in the production business. Summer finds each species of tree and flower in the process of producing its own unique contribution of fruit for the needs of man and beast. The blossoms that adorn the apple tree in springtime and fill the air with the breath of fragrance have fallen listlessly to the ground. The apple tree is not as pretty now in summertime. The green apples are expanding in size, expectant in promise, but still sour in taste and drab in color.

But as the summer days slip away, the world of nature is getting prepared for a fall festival. The trees and bushes that blanket the hillside start competing for the gaudiest attire. The red sumac and the while birch, the prickly locust and the sturdy oak, the hard hickory and the leafy elm—all take their turns strutting down the path of the autumn days attired in their most colorful clothes. God seems to have fun splashing crimsons and golds, copper reds and burnished bronzes across the canvas of nature.

As I watch this parade of seasons, I wonder if there are some themes running through it all. Is God trying to say something to His children by the way He closes out the growing season with a display of exquisite artistry? I believe there are lessons to be learned by studying this scene of autumnal splendor.

## The Joy of Achievement

Nature's most fruitful season is nature's most colorful season. The psalmist seems to sense this truth as he shouts: "Thou crownest the year with Thy bounty; the tracks of Thy chariot drip with fatness. The pastures of the wilderness drip, the hills gird themselves with joy, the meadows clothe themselves with flocks, the valleys deck themselves with grain, they shout and sing together for joy" (Ps. 65:11-13).

A fruit tree's reason for existence is to bear fruit. It has no claim to live if, exacting man's labor and the soil's fertility, it yields no harvest. The psalmist describes the man of God: "He is like a tree planted by the streams of water, that yields its fruit in its season" (Ps. 1:3). God is a creative God. After each act of creation in the Genesis account, it states, "And God saw that it was good." God applauds the achievement of accomplishment. When God put man into the garden, created in the image of God, there were tasks to do. Creative work was and is a blessing. Since the beginning, nature and man have thus celebrated the good harvest of worthwhile deeds.

Jesus told a parable in Luke 13 about a fig tree that bore no fruit. There was an exercise of patience, but there was also sternness. If the tree did not bear fruit after another year's opportunity, it would be cut down. Responsibility is the price of privilege. It is a warning to Christians who study apostolic history but never live apostolically. It is an indictment against hearing the Word and not doing it, of hearing the Gospel, but not bearing the fruits of the Spirit. Dag Hammarskjold said, "The road to holiness necessarily passes through action." Pious platitudes are not enough. Jesus said, "By their fruits you shall know them."

We are faced with the serious questions: "What are we trying to produce? and "Are we producing it?" There is an old legend of a man going to one of God's warehouses in heaven. He talked to the angel clerk about the lack of the fruits of the Spirit on the earth. The conversation rambled on over the ruin caused by pride, greed, indifference, injustice, and the like. The man told the clerk that the fruits of love, patience, kindness, and self-control were really in short supply and needed quickly, so he placed an order for some of this fruit. But the angel clerk told him, "I'm sorry, sir, but we don't carry any of this fruit in stock. We just have an inventory of seeds."

God operates something like that. He wants us to grow the seeds of possibility which He places within the soil of our lives, even as we sow seeds in the good earth on which He places us. He wants to share with us the excitement of growth and finally the thrill of the harvest. As Augustine said, "Without God we can not, without man God will not."

My father was a Sunday school teacher for many years before illness incapacitated him. He always had the senior high boys' class. He kept faithfully sowing the seed of God's Word Sunday after Sunday. Many years later during one of the ordination services at my home church a young man, about to enter the ministry, thanked the congregation for the support and nurture given to him during his growing years. He paused in his response, and then mentioned a few people who had shaped his life and encouraged him on his pathway to the parish. He mentioned his Sunday school teacher, my father! What joy there was in my father's heart. The harvest came when my father was still able to taste the fruits of his labor.

We were made to cultivate the new life created in us in our baptism and to develop and use the gifts of the Spirit. Jesus said, "I have come that they may have life, and have it abundantly" (John 10:10). So I can understand why nature puts on its bright clothes for the harvest festival.

The God of nature is celebrating. Likewise, the bulging bins and laden larders of Christian fruit-bearing should be cause for rejoicing.

## The Need for Deciduous Trees

As the colored leaves begin to cascade from the trees during an autumn breeze, there is a sadness as another growing season comes to a close. Nature seems to be naked except for the evergreen trees that refuse to shed their clothes. But the loss of leaves is a necessary part of growing and replenishing the forest soil. Those crimson and gold leaves of the deciduous trees now begin the process of decay.

The trees whisper their secrets to the mind of man. Man becomes aware that he, too, is a part of God's remarkable creation. The tree stands firm as the leaves fall. Man's faith, rooted in the promises of God, also stands firm as the leaves of new life replace the faded leaves of old habits and pious platitudes. There must always be a shedding of the past in order to make room for the sprouting of the buds of new life. This is another theme in the autumnal agenda.

This is a law of life and is very evident in the physical development of the body. Physiologists say that the body grows by death and rebirth of tissue. The body sloughs off its fingernails every few months. Eyebrows change every one hundred and fifty days. With the exception of the enamel on the teeth, the body replaces itself every seven years. Dr. Jessie Taft, in an article entitled "The Dynamics of Therapy in a Controlled Relationship," shows that this physical growth is typical of all growth: "At bottom all growth or change, like the birth process which is its prototype, is seen to contain the elements of death as well as life. As a rule the death aspect is only partial and is more than compensated for by the new life created thereby." In our baptism, we die daily and rise again to new life. For "we were buried with Christ by Baptism into death, that like as Christ rose from the dead, even we also should walk in newness of life."

To be deciduous like the tree is to discard, not destroy. To shake the leaves from the tree is far different than felling the tree itself. A faith that is deciduous, then, is one that discards ideas and behaviors which are no longer tenable. This, in no way, means the destruction of the tree of faith. This concept is not new.

Jesus talked about it in his Sermon on the Mount; He said, "Think not that I have come to abolish the Law and the prophets; I have not come to abolish them but to fulfil them" (Matt. 5:17). Rules and regulations were sometimes getting in the way of a real and vital relationship to Jesus Christ, the foundation and center of faith. People frequently want the security of old things no matter how outmoded they may be. But Paul says that "the new has come" in Jesus Christ (2 Cor. 5:17) "the old has passed away.

In the days of Jesus, the tree of Judaic faith was groaning under the weight of so many layers of leaves that it was necessary to shake some loose in order to prepare for a time of new greening. The church in every generation needs to grasp this principle of deciduousness. The church is not a monument to the past like the Egyptian pyramids. It is under orders to march under the banner and cross of Jesus Christ. There will always be times of shedding so there can be seasons of sprouting.

Paul talks about this process in his own life: "When I was a child, I spoke like a child, I thought like a child, I reasoned like a child; when I became a man, I gave up childish ways" (1 Cor. 13:11). Paul knew that understanding should be a matter of constant growth. He sought for the purposes and power of the resurrection to be lived out in his life. Nature gives us a clue to the dying and rising that is a part of real life.

## A Springtime Faith

A third theme that powerfully runs through the picture of autumn is this: death is not to be feared. Christ has broken its hold and conquered its curse. If the season of fall was the end of all life, I am sure God would have clothed the trees of hill and field with the black garments of mourning as they march their way to the grave. The contrary is true. Nature looks as though she is preparing for a wedding celebration. I wonder if God is saying to us, "Look! See! Learn about death from autumn's dress. The sunset trail is colorful because it points to the spring of salvation."

In farming communities we have all witnessed the planting of corn in the month of May. The seed must be buried in the soil if there is to be a fall harvest. The farmer does not succumb to despair when the seed is planted—gone from sight. Rather, he lives expectantly for the fruit of fall. Paul talks about the death of the child of God from this same viewpoint. He says, "So it is with the resurrection of the dead. What is sown is perishable, what is raised is imperishable. It is sown in dishonor, it is raised in glory. It is sown in weakness, it is raised in power. It is sown a physical body, it is raised a sprItual body" (1 Cor. 15:42-44).

Arthur Brisbane, a newspaper editor, wrote an Easter editorial which told the story of some caterpillars pulling an empty cocoon to its burial place. The caterpillars were dressed in black and weeping sadly. While they were on their long, sorrowful journey, above them floated the butterfly on bright, multicolored wings. While the caterpillars wept over the empty cocoon, the butterfly was rejoicing in its new freedom and life. Jesus said,

"I am the resurrection and the life; he who believes in Me, though he die, yet shall he live, and whoever lives and believes in Me shall never die" (John 11:25-26).

A Roman by the name of Seneca, who lived at the time of Christ, wrote: "Throughout our lives, we are making ourselves ready for another birth.... Therefore look forward without fear to that appointed hour—the last hour of the body, but not of the soul.... That day, which you fear as being the end of all things, is the birthday of your eternity." For those who are in Christ and in whom the risen Christ lives, this earthly life is a prolog to that glory which shall be revealed in us. Nature seems to have a birthday party as the colored leaves of autumn fall gently to the earth. It seems well aware that the hand of God will soon inevitably caress the creation with the springtime of new life and growth.

The eager earth waits for it to happen, and it always does. The resurrection of spring pronounces the same words of the resurrected Christ to the ageless question of Job, "If a man die, shall he live again." Surely he shall, as surely as day follows night, as surely as the stars follow their courses, as surely as spring follows the winter of fall, as surely as Easter follows Good Friday.

Oliver Cromwell, the famous English statesman, said to the mournful people surrounding his deathbed, "Will no one here thank God?" Perhaps the world of nature with its celebration of fall color is an expression of gratitude rather than grief as the winter season stands around the corner with its icy grip. The grasp of winter will not last long; neither will the journey through the valley of "the shadow of death." After that—eternal springtime.

So when a Christian dies, the mourners have our sincere sympathy; but just think of being a Christian, and

> Of stepping on shore,
>> And finding it heaven;
> Of taking hold of a hand,
>> And finding it God's hand;
> Of breathing new air,
>> And finding it celestial air;
> Of feeling invigorated,
>> And finding it immortality
> Of passing from storm and
>> tempest to an unbroken calm;
> Of waking up—
>> And finding it Home.
>> (Author unknown)

So autumn speaks and declares the glory of God. Nature's spirit is in tune with nature's God. God has done and shall do all things well. Stop, look, and listen to the themes on parade before your very eyes.

Jesus was sensitive to the splendor of his Father's world. While preaching in the meadow one day he said, "Consider the lilies of the field, how they grow; they neither toil nor spin; yet I tell you, even Solomon in all his glory was not arrayed like one of these. But if God so clothes the grass of the field, which today is alive and tomorrow is thrown into the oven, will he not much more clothe you, O men of little faith?" (Matt. 6:28-30). Peter, the big fisherman, heard that message in the meadow, and one day he wrote, "Cast all your anxieties on Him, for He cares about you" (1 Peter 5:7). May the lessons from nature also cause us to lean upon His everlasting arms.

### Parallel Scripture Reading

Psalm 1

### Suggested Hymns

O Beautiful for Spacious Skies
This Is My Father's World
For the Beauty of the Earth
We Praise Thee, O God, Our Redeemer, Creator

## LIVING AS CHRISTIANS UNDER AUSTERE CONDITIONS

### Seek the Lord and Live

AMOS 5:14-15

In his book *On a Clear Day You Can See General Motors,* John DeLorean describes the reasons why he felt conscience bound to quit his job at General Motors. His description of those reasons is summed up by this quotation taken from the excerpts published in the Minneapolis *Tribune,* March 7, 1980:

> There wasn't a man in top GM management who had anything to do with the Corvair who would purposely build a car that he knew would hurt or kill people. But, as part of a management team pushing for

increased sale and profits, each gave his individual approval in a group to decisions that produced the car in the face of serious doubts that were raised about its safety, and then later sought to squelch information that might prove the car's deficiencies.

This quotation sums up the pressures big business can place on the individual to sacrifice his soul for the sake of making a profit. Individually, the decision would not have been made, but corporately, it was made. Similarly, some of the major oil companies were recently fined for charging too much for their product. The corporation was found guilty, but who was individually responsible we'll probably never know. Corporate bigness hides the individual's accountability.

### Seek the Lord in Right Thoughts

According to the prophet Amos these examples illustrate that big business in our day is often similar to the type of business conducted in Israel eight centuries before Christ. In chapter 8, Amos accuses the businessmen of his day of waiting eagerly for the Sabbath day to get over, so they could go back to cheating their customers, not just one way but several ways at once. But dishonest business practices were only a part of Amos' castigation of the society of his day. He also attacked the law courts of his day which meted out justice to the highest bidder and ignored the one who sought real justice at its hands. Often we hear the charge made today that justice is based on how high priced a lawyer one can afford, and sentences are determined by one's economic status rather than by the merits or demerits of the case at issue. Here the example is often cited of Nixon's assistants who spent minimal terms in jails that featured the most liberal policies during confinement. They went to "white collar" jails not the "blue collar" type. Amos also attacked the religious practices of his day. People went to the local shrine every Sabbath, but Amos attacked them for mere formalism and failure to actually live the religion they claimed to practice. Finally, Amos rebuked the class distinctions in society. The rich got richer at the expense of the poor and the oppressed, and trampled on them and their rights. They built fancy homes and cabins on the lake and spent their time in idle luxury at the expense of the poor. Eighth-century Israel was an age of luxury and decadence, whose closest parallel can be found in our society today in America. It was an age which could not conceive of the idea that the wealth, the food, the drink, the fancy homes, and the winter palaces could be removed, could be destroyed, could be wiped out by a total national disaster. It was an age that could not conceive of practicing national austerity.

To that age Amos makes the plea in our text. Seek the good and live. Hate evil and love the good and not vice versa. It's a call to repentance, to change their way of living and "Maybe—maybe," the prophet said, "God would be gracious to the remnant of Joseph." The maybe was not because Amos thought it likely God would not be gracious, but because Amos could not be sure of the response by the people of his day to the appeal to repent. And Amos' doubts proved accurate. Some 20—30 years later the luxury, the idle rich, and Israel itself, were all gone, destroyed because of the unrepented lack of justice and righteousness which characterized its society's way of life.

In Luke 13 we find a similar call to repentance issued by Jesus. Here Jesus points to a couple of tragedies that had recently occurred in his day and asks the question, "Did these tragedies happen because the people killed were more guilty than we?" "No," He says, "but unless you repent, you will all likewise perish." The point Jesus made was that tragedy is not to be used as a chance for us to condemn others but rather as a warning to us that tragedy strikes any one and any time suddenly, unexpectedly, and sometimes fatally. So we need to be prepared to face the unexpected—whether national disaster as in Amos' day, or unexpected tragedy—as in Jesus' day; and the Christian's preparation is to repent—to seek the Lord and live, in the words of Amos.

### Seek the Lord in Good Work

In Luke 13 Jesus explains what it means to seek the Lord and live—to repent—in the parable of the fig tree. It was green. It was healthy. It was strong and sturdy. There was nothing wrong with it, except it had produced no fruit. That fig tree was much like a healthy, strong, sturdy, muscular, 6-foot, 20th-century American. Outwardly there seems to be nothing wrong with him, but what kind of fruit is he producing? The owner wanted to destroy that fig tree for wasting valuable nutrients in the soil and taking up valuable space, but the gardener begged that it be given one more chance. He would dig around it and fertilize it and then maybe it would produce the fruit the owner sought the next year.

"Hear the grace of God in the parable," Amos might say. There is one more chance for the unproductive fig tree, and "maybe" it will produce fruit. The maybe is because of the fig tree, not because of the owner or the gardener. Amos pleaded with the people of his day to take the one more chance offered them before it was too late. Jesus reminded the hearers of his day not to delay the grasping of that chance—"unless you repent you will all likewise perish." The grace of God grants us that one more chance—we who are those fine, healthy, 6-foot , 20th-century Americans, but failure to accept that one more chance leads to the judgment, the punishment, the destruction.

But God does all he can to prevent its happening. The gardener dug and fertilized. One sermon writer described it this way; he dug out the weeds of sin and broke up the clods of self-righeousness and manured the tree with the Gospel—offensive though it smelled, yet it had the nutrients needed to produce the fruit called repentance from that fig tree. That's the grace of God at work around us and for us to bring forth from us the fruit he seeks. God seeks to bring about our repentance.

And in Amos' day? God had dug and manured plenty, Amos tells us. He had sent famine, but yet they had failed to return to the Lord. And in our day? God is still digging and manuring. We had a trucker strike last summer that threatened the food supply in the Twin Cities and last week a meat cutters strike that closed at least one major food market chain. Did we return to the Lord in the middle of a short food supply, recognizing that He is, provider of our daily bread, or did we fail to hear ignoring the whole thing? God sent drought, Amos said, and yet they failed to return to the Lord. Three years ago the Twin Cities went through a similar drought. Was it taken as a warning to check our relationship with God or only as a passing natural phenomenon? Israel in the 8th century failed to respond to God's digging and manuring. How do we respond today to similar tragedies used by God to call us back to Himself? God sent blight and mildew and grasshoppers in Amos' day and today. Grasshoppers appeared again in a plague in the western parts of our country last summer. How did we respond? God sent disease and war, Amos said, and still the people of his day failed to return. Is 20th-century America that different from 8th century (B.C.) Israel? Is the response the same or is it different? Do we seek the Lord and live or fail to return? Do we repent of our ways or fail to heed those warning calls of His grace? God did all He could in 8th-century Israel to bring about a repentant return. He is still doing all He can today to bring about a repentant return in 20th-century America.

In the '80s, we are told, we face a declining supply of oil and gas, necessary items for our country's welfare. We face unknown shortages of food, of shelter, of clothing in various parts of our globe. We face wars and the threats of war. We face 20 percent inflation in 1980 alone and 20 percent interest rates or higher very soon. And in the midst of our declining prosperity and rising need to practice austerity, we need to hear first the voice of Amos, "Seek the Lord and live," or of Jesus, "Unless you repent, you will all likewise perish." God is still calling us just as He has in the past, to respond to His Word with heartfelt contrition, confession of our sins, trust in His forgiveness, and the promise to serve God totally with our lives in the difficult days ahead.

Recently the papers carried an article describing how the Minnesota Motor Boat Association was demanding that motor boats be exempt from any future gas rationing plans. Some will refuse to hear God's call. Some fig trees will need to be cut down in their prime for failure to produce fruit. Perhaps that is why the verse preceding our text, apparently a wisdom saying quoted by Amos, says in times like these the wise keep silent. They keep silent to survive, it seems to imply. But Amos couldn't keep silent, and Jesus didn't in His day. The reason? Because the grace of God needs to be heard. God would call us to repent, to seek Him and find in Him life—real life, full life. The hymn writer wrote, "Seek where ye may to find a way that leads to your salvation. My heart is stilled. On Christ I build." 20th-century America like 8th-century Israel offers literally hundreds of saving products, but none can survive the austere times ahead. Only in Christ can we find the deliverance we seek: deliverance that leads to life and salvation.

### Seek the Lord in Repentance and Faith

Amos' call to seek the Lord and live is a call for us to reevaluate our whole lives. Our lives need to be reevaluated at work—how often do we sacrifice our conscience for the profit motive? Is our motivation just to keep our job because we cannot face the austere alternative? We need to reevaluate our lives at school—are we there to learn or just to get entertained? At home—what happens in the family? Does it exist together or does it live and grow together? Our play—vacation time—is it seeking the Lord to drive 5—10-mile-a-gallon campers, or to run motor boats purely for pleasure? Are we revising our way of life? Is it not in that life that the fruits of repentance are to be offered?

Amos failed to find evidences of repentance and change in the lives of 8th-century Israelites. So he had to say "maybe." Maybe God will be gracious if only you hear His call this one last time. Today we hear the same call; the call to reevaluation, to repentance. It contains in it the power to accomplish the change. In it is the power of God at work through our Lord and Savior Jesus Christ. That power led Him to the cross. That power raised Him from the dead. That power would give us life in His name. "Seek the Lord and live," Amos said. "Let the tree live," the gardener said. "Let that healthy, 6-foot, American live," God would say. But let him live in the power of Christ and in the name of Jesus. Let him live by the grace of God.

God is giving us another chance to seek Him in the austere days ahead, to change our wasteful ways and to live in Him. That chance is found in His Son, our Lord and Savior Jesus Christ. The grace of God is such that He surrounds us with the fertilizer of the Gospel, which contains the nutritious power we need to change from decadent luxury to austere stewardship. The Gospel is the good news of Jesus Christ our Savior. He died that we might live. He offers us life in His own name. Seek the Lord—the Lord Jesus Christ, and live!

### Parallel Scripture Readings

| | | | |
|---|---|---|---|
| Psalm 130 | Amos 5:4-15 | Ephesians 4:17-25 | Luke 13:1-9 |
| Amos 4:6-12 | Isaiah 5:1-8 | Philippians 2:12-18 | |

### Suggested Hymns

The Lord Hath Helped Me Hitherto
Seek Where Ye May to Find a Way
My Spirit on Thy Care
My Soul, Be on Thy Guard
I Lay My Sins on Jesus


## LIVING AS CHRISTIANS UNDER AUSTERE CONDITIONS

### Trust in the Lord for Daily Bread

JOHN 6:1-15


The trouble with this miracle from the American point of view is that it is not told from the American point of view. If this were an American miracle story, there would not have been 5,000 people fed by five loaves of bread and two small fish. Instead, there would have been a small select number of people fed a magnificent repast of countless delightful varieties of food and drink and served in an intimate quiet setting. That would be an American version of this story, because the American view of food has been that it is a luxury item rather than a necessity of life. If the average American had been present on the mountain that day when Jesus fed that crowd, he would at least have expected tartar sauce for the fish, ham and cheese on the bread, and a nice cold beer to wash it all down. Failing all that, he would certainly have complained about the poor quality and variety of the food which Jesus had provided, probably would have gotten up without leaving the disciples a tip, and walked out. Bread and fish is just not our idea of a special meal. It's something you get at McDonald's when you get tired of Big Macs and cheeseburgers.

### What Is Daily Bread?

The story of the feeding of the 5,000 is almost so well known to us that it is meaningless to us. We know the details of the story so well that we are probably more often bored by hearing it read again as a lesson than we are interested in what the story has to convey to us. Yet when we live in an age of belt tightening, the question of one's daily bread becomes more than just a luxury item. For many it becomes (to coin a terrible pun) a real gut issue. And precisely because we are so used to having our daily needs met in the ways described above, with plenty of variety and a variety of plenty, we are apt to think like the crowd in the lesson when we are confronted with a situation where that daily need is going to be difficult if not impossible to meet.

They were away from home. Food was not close by. Yet something needed to be done. And Jesus did something. He provided for their need. But note the reaction of the crowd at the end of the lesson. They were going to come by force to make Jesus king. The crowd had fallen prey to a common temptation—the type of temptation to which we could very easily succumb. The temptation is to misbelieve on the basis of what we know God can and does do to provide for our daily needs. The crowd had seen the sign Jesus had just done. They knew what that sign meant. They said, "This is the prophet who is to come into the world." They interpreted the sign as an indication that the Messianic age had dawned, that Jesus was the Messiah or at least the forerunner of the Messiah. And they were right, at least partly right, but they came to the wrong conclusion. They tried to make Him into their idea of the prophet who was to come—an earthly king—and that was their misbelief.

Just what is misbelief? It is believing. However, it is believing that is twisted. It's an insidious form of idolatry, because it is an unconscious and very often "innocent" way of making God in our image, of attempting to mold God to fit our pattern of thought, of making God act the way we want Him to act and at the time we want Him to act. Misbelief acts very much like cancer. It's the gradual replacement of healthy cells by cancerous cells. At first, nothing seems to be wrong. Very often, there is only a slight discomfort felt with one's misbelief but if ignored it goes away. Gradually, the situation gets worse, and it can reach that critical point where the healthy cells can no longer survive. Finally, it can get out of control and, if drastic action is not taken, become fatal. That is misbelief.

That is the type of temptation we face in the coming days of less prosperity and greater austerity. It will be easy to let our faith, our trust be twisted by economic misfortunes, by declining savings, by the loss of a job, by failure to keep up with inflation—twisted into the belief that somehow, the problem lies in God. It may be twisted to the point that my trust of God somehow implies that He has to provide for my daily needs in the manner to which I have become accustomed. Somehow, my faith means a full stomach, staying ahead of inflation, keeping my job and getting an advance in rank, increasing my savings and economic security in a time of economic hardship or disaster. But that is twisted faith, misbelief. It is acting like the crowd in the text. It's making God into our image of what He should be and forcing Him to act the way we think He should. It's thinking He must provide us with the tartar sauce, the mustard, french fries, and a cold beer, instead of just plain bread and some small and slightly smelly fish.

### Who Provides Daily Bread?

The two disciples in the story, Philip and Andrew, demonstrate another form of misbelief. Jesus put the problem in their laps—how are we going to feed this crowd? Philip could only think of finding enough money to buy food for the crowd, but he knew that was a hopeless situation. Andrew at least found a lad with some food, but he knew it too was hopeless. There wasn't nearly enough to go around. This kind of misbelief tries to use its faith to accomplish the work of God. It recognizes the problem, and it searches for the solution, but due to misbelief, it looks for the solution inside itself. It looks to its own resources for the answer and, finding them hopelessly inadequate, gives up and says nothing can be done. In other words, this kind of misbelief finds its hope in having the resources ready at hand within reach to solve the problem. When those resources fail, when they are difficult to find, when the austerity of life shows them to be insufficient, it can do nothing else but say, "It's hopeless. Nothing can be done."

But this miracle story is a reminder to us that the situation is not hopeless. Something can be done, but we need to look to Jesus for the solution—not that we expect Him to miraculously solve our daily needs by becoming a sugar daddy or bread king. To think the situation hopeless is the disciples' form of misbelief. To look for a sugar daddy is the crowd's form of misbelief. Instead we need to trust that Jesus can and will provide for our daily needs. That too is a miracle. That we are fed by God from the hand of Jesus in the smallest things of life is miraculous. He does provide, not always the way we would like, not often in the quantity we would like, not even in the variety we would like, but He does provide, and He satisfies our needs. He fed the 5,000—every one of them. He provides for us too, still more than most of us need, as with the 5,000, so that there are usually leftovers to be put in the refrigerated baskets for the next day.

In this time of rising need it is easy for us to assume that God does not care, that He does not notice, that He is not there. When needs go unfilled, it is easy, it is human, it is common to blame God. But this miracle story assures us that God does notice and He does care. It was Jesus who noticed the need of the crowd for food. It was Jesus who met that need and provided for it. He provided for it through a young boy's lunch. For us perhaps it will be a friend who loans us $50 when we need it most. Perhaps it will be a relative who pulls us through—a father who helps us get over the difficulties of starting to farm, a brother who gives us some good advice, or perhaps it will be a stranger we will never meet again. Perhaps it will be a debt we couldn't pay that will be forgiven. The point is that God will provide for our needs just as in the past, through those whom we meet in our daily life, just as Jesus used that lunch to provide for the need of the crowd.

## Where Is the Blessing?

The prophet Jonah wanted God to destroy Nineveh, and he got very angry when its people repented and God spared the city instead. But God told him in the last verse of the book, "Should not I pity Nineveh, that great city in which there are more than a hundred and twenty thousand persons who do not know their right hand from their left, and also much cattle?" God was concerned not only for the human life in that city but even for the animal life as well. Earlier God had shown that same concern in the days of Noah when he made a covenant, not only with Noah and his family but also with the animals, never to destroy all life with a flood again. Or in the Sermon on the Mount Jesus says, "look at the birds of the air; they neither sow nor reap nor gather into barns, and yet your heavenly Father feeds them." God cares so much for the animals, and Jesus then asks the question that puts that care into perspective for us: "Are you not of more value then they?" If God provides for the animals (plants too one could add), He will certainly also provide for us.

The psalmist said, "The eyes of all wait for You, O Lord, and You give them their food in due season. You open Your hand and satisfy the desire of every living thing." God does care—that we need to know, believe, and hear when our needs seem to go unfilled. He will provide—that we can believe and trust. He opens His hand and provides for every living thing.

The hand of God—that was the sign the people saw that day. But they took the hand and wanted to use it their way. The hand of God is still at work today touching the common and everyday things of this life like that young boy's lunch. It touches them in such a way that miracles still take place. Astonishingly, when we think the situation hopeless, we are still fed and have some left over. Amazingly, when we want to use God for our ends, He turns it around and uses us for His ends, and it works out better than we had imagined that way. God provides today as then. He sends His rain on the just and the unjust, the psalmist said. He opens His hand and satisfies the desire of every living thing. That's not misbelief talking. That's faith talking. Faith sees the hand of God and recognizes it and believes and trusts. Faith takes hold of the hand of God and is led. It does not try to lead. Faith clings to the hand of God and is fed. Faith trusts the hand of God for its daily bread.

The hand of God must always remain the hand of God. It can never be twisted by misbelief into becoming the hand of man. Faith trusts that God will provide, in His own time and in His own way. Faith follows where God's hand leads, and God's hand never leads astray. That's the Gospel in the Gospel. God provides for our daily needs, even in times of want. He still provides. Trust in God. Cling to His hand and follow where He leads. (One could conclude the sermon by asking the congregation to rise and say together Ps. 23.)

### Parallel Scripture Readings

Psalms 23, 40, 91
1 Kings 17:1-16 or 1 Kings 18:7-16
Philippians 4:10-13 or James 4:13-16
John 6:1-15

### Suggested Hymns

The King of Love My Shepherd Is
O God of Mercy, God of Might
I Leave All Things to God's Direction
Rejoice My Heart, Be Glad and Sing
My Soul Now Bless Thy Maker

## LIVING AS CHRISTIANS
## UNDER AUSTERE CONDITIONS

## Live in the Lord and Rejoice

HABAKKUK 3:17-18

The scene is 1941 in Great Britain. U-boats began to take their toll of merchant shipping, and wartime rationing began to pinch. Food grew scarce, and each person was limited to one pound of meat per week, four pounds of canned beans a week. Milk was seven pints per week for children and expectant mothers. Others got half that much. Since meat was scarce, newspapers and government agencies printed recipes for meatless or near meatless dishes. One was called a carrot casserole and consisted of the following: 3 carrots, 1 heaped teaspoonful of salt, ½ flat tablespoonful of pepper, 1 tablesppon brown sugar, 1 flat teaspoonful of ground ginger, 3 potatoes and 1 onion if available. Another recipe was something called patriotic pudding which consisted of 8 oz. of flour, 2 oz. grated raw potato, 2 oz. suet, a pinch of salt and just enough cold water to make soft dough. This was spread with 1 lb. chopped root vegetables, salt, pepper, and diced bacon or gravy powder. This was enough to feed four people so that they "would have energy and vitamins in a way they will like." (Henry Adams, *Years of Deadly Peril* [New York: David McKay Co. Inc. 1969] p. 461.)

That's life in austere times. One wonders whether the average American will experience the same austerity in another year (I'm writing in April 1980). But at least it gives us some point of comparison for our life now. How could people survive on that diet? How can we survive on our diets now? How could people eat that way? How can we continue to eat the way we do now? Inflation, high interest rates, the silver market gone mad (the Hunt family just lost a bundle on the silver market); are we on a roller coaster from the prosperity of the 70's to extreme poverty in the 80's? No one knows. God knows, but He's not telling. How do we face life when it seems to be dark, foreboding, cloudy ahead, and no sign of relief in sight?

### Life's Minimal Needs

The prophet Habakkuk knew. He too faced cloudy days ahead. He saw a bitter and hasty nation on the horizon preparing to march on his tiny kingdom. He saw them riding swift horses, coming for violence, scoffing at kings and fortresses, sweeping by like the wind. He saw the Chaldeans coming soon against little Judah, and he cried out to God. Why? Was his not a more righteous people than they? How could this be happening to them? What was God doing anyway?

Just what is God doing today? A recent article describing victims of inflation told how one young family with four children simply couldn't make ends meet any more. Four-year-old son Brian needed surgery to repair a cleft palate, and it cost $1,500. Insurance covered some of the cost, but the parents' couldn't pay the rest. The father's salary was enough for food and rent and that's all. The parents have a 10th-grade education. They used to go out for a beer together to the corner bar, but can't afford it any more. What is God doing anyway? Is this fair? I mean, America is a more righteous nation than other nations, isn't it?

Habakkuk got an answer to his complaint. It was a plain answer written clearly on tablets. Greed is like death. It never gets enough. The arrogant man does not survive—the one who heaps up what is not his own and loads himself with pledges. His debtors will rise against him, but the righteous man will live by his faithfulness. That was the answer given the prophet Habakkuk, "the righteous lives by his faithfulness." Faithfulness is loyalty to God because we have confidence in Him. It's confidence in spite of what's happening in one's daily life, not because of what's happening in one's daily life. Faithfulness is loyalty to God when things go wrong, not when things go right. Harvest failure, drought, famine, nothing will prevent the prophet from rejoicing in the Lord God of His salvation. Paul said it again in Romans, "Who shall separate us from the love of Christ? Shall tribulation or distress or famine or peril or nakedness or sword? In all these things we are more than conquerors through Him who loved us."

And that is the answer for us in trying times, when the means of obtaining this world's goods seem farther from our reach each and every day. The answer is trust in the Lord. Trust only in Him, not in self, not in things, not in wealth, not in accumulation of property, not in military might, not in clever diplomacy or the ability to outwit one's creditors. Trust in the Lord and rejoice in Him. The strangest thing about this text is that Habakkuk says not only that he will trust in the Lord in trying situations, but he will rejoice in Him too. That seems like the height of idiocy—even beyond the limits of foolishness. If God was fair and worth trusting, would He not make things better and easier for us in life and give us reason to rejoice in Him?

The answer, the prophet knew, was that He has done all this. The answer, Paul knew, was that He has fulfilled all this in Christ. He has become our salvation. He has done what was needed to deliver us from all troubles, from every evil, and Paul gives quite a list—from even those things in life that seem totally unfair, unjust, and undeserved as Habakkuk described in chapter 1. But trust trusts nevertheless, Luther said. It trusts despite what is happening. Trust needs no crutches. Trust is the confidence that God is the one who worked out my salvation, my deliverance, my rescue, and help for my condition. Trust relies on what God has done in Jesus Christ and on that alone. "He is our refuge and strength, a very present help in trouble," the psalm writer said, and, furthermore, he believed and trusted that though the earth would be removed or the mountains shake in the heart of the sea, though the waters roar and foam, God would still be a place of refuge, shelter, security, and safety in time of trouble. He is a saving God no matter what the present situation in our daily life seems to say to the contrary.

## God Above Everything

So how are we to live in the difficult days ahead? We are to live as always in the Lord. That means we are to take seriously the First Commandment to place God first in our lives, to fear, love, and trust in Him above everything else and everyone else. That is possible because of Christ. We can do it only because God showed His love to us first in Jesus Christ. He died that we might live in Him. Through His death and resurrection we live and move and have our being. Through Him the First Commandment is and can be kept in our lives. Through Him we can live in Him. And we can then say, "Inflation I defy you. High interest rates I laugh at you. Fear, I bid you cease." We can say that because we live in the Lord God who has saved.

And we can rejoice in those difficult days ahead living in the Lord God. Our happiness has not come to an end with $1.25 gas or higher, with a smaller house than what we wanted to buy, with a smaller savings account in the bank, with a less expensive vacation, with the loss of one's cabin on the lake, or the inability to afford the higher quality product as before. Our happiness is not based on that. Austerity, prosperity, that is not what determines that joyous expectation with which we look forward to each new dawn. As Christians that is determined by that one thing necessary— the part that Mary chose—because it's best. Trust in the Lord God, the Father of Mary's teacher, our Lord and Savior Jesus Christ. We can rejoice in that fact because that we have not lost; that we cannot lose. It is ours by faith. It is the part which cannot be taken away from Mary or from us. It is our salvation.

Did you ever notice how little children get all those expensive toys at Christmas time or for their birthdays? How do they react? They unwrap them and play with them for a little while, but later the children play more with the wrapping paper or with the boxes the toys came in than the toys themselves. And those kids are happy that way. How much of the trouble, the unhappiness, the fear, despair, worry, and load weighing down upon our shoulders isn't just that? Somehow we got used to being happy with more than the wrapping paper and boxes. And how much of it isn't because we forgot what happiness is? Charles Schulze has written many books to remind us that happiness is found not where we plan for it, look for it, or think it to be, but more often it is around when we are not looking, planning, or striving for it but simply living the life our Creator meant us to live. When we live in the Lord, happiness is found because that is the way we were created to live. Happiness is ours as a possession that comes with that life.

Homemade ice cream always tastes better than the "boughten" kind. So does homemade bread, homemade soup, homemade doughnuts, homemade pies, and cakes. Why is that? It's because there's nothing artifical about it. There's nothing artifical about life in the Lord either. To discover it is to find peace. To live it is to experience joy. To rejoice in it is to really live.

The scene is 1981 in America. Inflation, high-interest rates, climbing unemployment; will that be the picture? Habakkuk says it doesn't matter. Though the situation be ever so bad, worse than I could imagine now in April 1980, yet we can rejoice in the Lord, because he is the God of our salvation. Carrot casseroles and patriotic puddings may be revived or they may not. It's not important. What is important is knowing we can still rejoice because God still saves as he did in Habakkuk's day. That means we can live. Live in the Lord and rejoice.

### Parallel Scripture Readings

Psalms 92,116                          Acts 3:1-10
Habakkuk 3:17-18                       Acts 5:27-42
Philippians 4:4-7 or Romans 8:31-39

### Suggested Hymns

Through All the Changing Scenes of Life
What Is the World to Me?
O God of Mercy, God of Might
What God Ordains Is Always Good

Lord, It Belongs Not to My Care
What Our Father Does Is Well


# FAMILIES: WHOLE OR BROKEN

## Living with Your Family and Friends

1 CORINTHIANS 16:20


"All the brethren send greetings. Greet one another with a holy kiss." What kind of a feeling do you get when you hear these words of Paul? For many of us in North America, kissing is connected with romance. It's what people who are in love do. Or it's what parents do to show that they love their children, especially when the children are small. Mother says, "Give me a big kiss." And baby comes toddling over to plant a wet, well-intentioned kiss on her face.

But there may come a time when that show of affection is a source of embarrassment. That was demonstrated at an eighth-grade graduation where a mother tried to give her son a kiss as she proudly handed him his diploma. He quickly, emphatically turned his head away from her. There was a little giggle that rippled through the audience as they saw this show of modesty and mild rejection. After that few parents tried to reward their children with a kiss.

Our theme is "Living with Your Family and Friends." In that little display between parent and child the young man saw that there had to be some distance between himself and his family in front of all those people and in front of his friends. What happened was an example of the conflict that often develops as a youngster tries to walk the tightrope between family and friends.

### The Symbol of Closeness

For him, the kiss, a symbol of love, became a symbol of something else. Probably all of us have been in a situation where we were forced to show affection in public when we really didn't want to. That happens, but the sad thing is that it may also indicate a basic separation between friends and family which God never intended for us.

When God created us, it was so that we could praise Him and live together in harmony with our families and our friends. He breathed life into Adam and Eve and made it possible for them to share that holy kiss that Paul speaks of. And yet we have gone so far from that kiss of peace.

### To Dispel Loneliness

One of the big problems of our society is loneliness. Adam had a sense of alone-ness before Eve was created, even though he was in tune with the animals around him and with all of nature. As Eve came into his life, he had a sense of completeness. But, oh, how they must have been overcome with their own aloneness as they fell into sin and found that they were cut off from God and from each other. Much of that loneliness lingers with us today.

Sometimes we think of people who live alone as being the most lonely individuals around. That's not necessarily true. There are lonely children living in what we would call complete families. There are lonely married people and lonely singles. There are people who are lonely in crowds, at parties, in church. Paul had a sense of loneliness as he thought of all the friends who had deserted him. And that sense of loneliness can overcome an individual.

So it's important that we realize that it was not God's plan for us to be alone. He placed us in families and made it possible for us to have friends. We have to realize that we cause the problems in God's plan. But his plan for us is still the same. In Christ, we live with our families and our friends. Jesus said that He never had a permanent home; but as we look at what we know about His life, we see that He certainly had family and He certainly had friends. Even as He went off by Himself to pray, He was not really alone. He took friends along with Him. Granted, those friends fell asleep instead of watching with Him, and they ran off on Him. Still, He never deserted them. And that's the important point, He has never deserted us.

### To Combat Sins That Separate

Adam and Eve must have been filled with such hope after God picked them up when they had fallen. Think how they must have felt after Cain killed Abel. And how Cain felt. We know something about that. He was to be banished as a fugitive and a wanderer on the earth (Gen. 4:12). Even though he had killed his brother, the thought of being exiled from his family was overpowering to him. And so he said to God, "My punishment is greater than I can bear. Behold, Thou hast driven me this day away from the ground; and from Thy face I shall be hidden; and I shall be a fugitive and a wanderer on the earth. And whoever finds me will slay me" (Gen. 4:13-14). Being cut off from the presence of his family was also, in his mind, going to cut him off from the presence of God and any security that he had.

What we are told about Cain though after he is exiled is that he started his own family. As we move through Scripture, we see God dealing with family after family because it is always part of His plan—to have people relate to each other and to Him through family and friends.

## The Symbol of Unity

There was a certain unity among people, which continued until the people united against God decided to build the Tower of Babel as a monument to themselves and their own power. Then God broke them up into separate language units, and they went their own separate ways. And to this day we are set apart by differences in our language or speech and by special words that we use. We can never say though that it is God who has caused the divisions among us. We have done it ourselves by setting ourselves against Him.

We see that division among the Corinthians to whom Paul writes, "Greet one another with a holy kiss." Those were people with problems as severe as any we will ever encounter. They had even divided themselves within the church according to whom they thought they should give their loyalty. Some claimed to be followers of Paul and some claimed to be followers of Apollos. Paul had to remind them that they did not find life in him or in Apollos. Rather, they had life in Jesus. Instead of greeting each other with that holy kiss signifying their unity, they were dividing up as if they were warring factions.

## To Avoid Taking Sides

Think of how may times you have chosen sides and divided into a "we—they" position where others in your family or among your friends were outsiders instead of being brothers and sisters.

An attempt to break down the "we—they" has been the kiss of peace, which in many places has simply been turning to the person in the pew next to you, shaking hands, and saying something like "peace be with you." A woman who was not used to shaking hands in church remarked, "I only shake hands with people that I like and people that I know. I certainly don't go to church to shake hands with a bunch of strangers."

## To Act as Christian Brothers and Sisters

That's not the view of the church Paul had in mind when he sent a word of greeting from Christians in one place to Christians in another. He sees the church, even with its problems, as a group of families and friends gathering in the name of Jesus. The idea of the holy kiss is fitting because it signifies all of the love that we feel for one another in Christ.

Remember again, those Christians to whom Paul wrote had every kind of problem imaginable. To him, they were Christian brothers and sisters, important because of and in spite of who they were.

Carry that attitude over to your life with your family and friends, and you will be reflecting the attitude and way of life which will help you live with those around you.

Jesus told His friends, "This is My commandment, that you love one another as I loved you. Greater love has no man than this, that a man lay down his life for his friends" (John 15:12-13). That is, of course, what He did, laid down His life for those friends and for us. Having a friend means that you are willing to give yourself for that friend.

### The Symbol of Sacrifice

There have been great love stories and stories of friendships where one person sacrificed himself for the other. And there have been stories where both have been willing to die for the sake of their love. There is only one story that has shown any lasting consistency though. It has lasted through all of the years since the Fall into sin. That is the story of the love of God shown to us through Jesus Christ.

So often what is reflected to us is the example of casual relationships which allow people to drift from friendship to friendship and from marriage to marriage. And a kiss can be the kind of kiss that Judas gave to Jesus—not a kiss which says, "You are important to me," but rather a kiss which says, "I want to use you."

### To See Christ in Life and Death

The other kind of kiss is possible. It is possible because Jesus makes it possible. He shows us what it means to share with people. Think of Jesus weeping at the grave of Lazarus. Certainly, He didn't weep simply because Lazarus had died. He had delayed long enough so that Lazarus would be dead in order for Him to show the people what was to come—to show them that He had power over life and death. He wept because of the hurt that Mary and Martha felt at the loss of their brother. He wept because they wept.

In many ways, we are oriented toward simple answers and simple kinds of solutions. We would like to be able to say in this situation it is best if you respond this way or that way. However, life doesn't always confront us with the simple problems. One response may not fit every kind of life setting.

There is a lot of uncertainty about day-to-day existence, and yet we can find a lot of certainty as we face the day in Christ and as we come together with our family and friends in Christ. Living with your family and your friends means greeting them with a holy kiss. It does not mean playing one off against the other. Of course, at times you may have to emphasize the welfare of one over the welfare of the other. But if you always find that you are having to make a choice between family or friends, it is probably time to look at what is happening in your life.

### To Share with People

Remember that as sinner and saint, living among sinners and saints, there will always be the need to look into the mirror of the Law, which demands repentance, and at the same time to share the word of forgiveness, which is ours in Christ. And through all of life runs the thread of God's love, which makes it possible for us to love and to live with family and friends.

Have you ever watched a little child at play suddenly experience some pain? That child will immediately run to the parent or person who takes care of him or her. Nobody else can provide comfort at that moment. And by the same token, when the child is filled with joy, he or she will run to that same care-giver. That is a sample of what it means to live with family and friends. It means to be able to share the hurts and the joys without fear of being rejected.

In Christ, share those hurts and joys. And each day greet one another with a holy kiss.

### Parallel Scripture Readings

Philippians 1:1-11     John 13:3-15       Matthew 19:21 ff.
Ephesians 6:1-4        Matthew 22:34-40   Luke 10:25 ff.

### Suggested Hymns

What a Friend We Have in Jesus
Christ Is Our Cornerstone
Jesus, Jesus, Only Jesus
Let Us Ever Walk with Jesus
A Mighty Fortress Is Our God

# FAMILIES: WHOLE OR BROKEN

## Divorce

MATTHEW 19:3-9

Today's message is about divorce. It's based on the words of our Lord in the gospels, especially in Matt. 19:3-9. It says, "The Pharisees came up to Him and tested Him by asking, 'Is it lawful to divorce one's wife for any cause?' He answered, 'Have you not read that He who made them from the beginning made them male and female?' And [He] said, 'For this reason a man shall leave his father and mother and be joined to his wife, and the two shall become one. So they are no longer two but one. What therefore God has joined together, let no man put asunder.' They said to Him, 'Why then did Moses command one to give a certificate of divorce and to put her away?' He said to them, 'For your hardness of heart Moses allowed you to divorce your wives, but from the beginning it was not so. And I say to you, whosoever divorces his wife, except for unchastity, and marries another commits adultery.'"

This is not an easy subject to speak on in only a very few minutes and especially in a one-way fashion where not everything can be said or every situation considered. Yet it is necessary, because this is one of the few arenas in life where the church gets to address itself to a growing contemporary concern.

### Its Causes

In speaking on this subject, please let it be understood from the outset that I am not pointing the finger at any one individual, couple, or family. People who have gone through the tragedy of divorce need our help and understanding. We all need to hear about this since there is hardly a family unit among us that somewhere among the relatives has not been affected by the reality of broken marriages, separation, and divorce.

Some people have said to their pastor, or to a friend, or maybe even to a parent, "I didn't want a divorce, but the marriage had already died." Others have said, "I didn't want a divorce, but my spouse went ahead and got one anyhow." And still others have said, "I didn't want a divorce. I'm against it because of my understanding of the Bible and of God's will for my life, but I had to. I had to get a divorce. My spouse compelled me. I had to do it for the sake of my own mental health and physical well-being."

Divorce presently affects at least one out of every four marriages in the United States. No marriage is immune. And almost always, divorce leaves a trail of pain and problems for lots and lots of people. It hardly ever affects only a husband and wife, only one man and woman.

So, what's the problem? People often ask. And some suggest that it's differing backgrounds. Maybe. Could it be unreasonable and unreachable expectations of marriage? Sometimes. Money? In my experience it's often too much rather than too little! Maybe it's lack of support and encouragement from family and friends, from society and from the media? Quite often that plays a part. Perhaps the problem is a poor sex life? Sometimes. Unwillingness to grow, to change? A lack of ability to listen or to talk or to communicate? Occasionally that's true. Emotional problems or personality disorders? Once in a while that happens. Perhaps we do not have sufficient training or good modeling for marriage? Surely that's a part. Misuse of alcohol and drugs? With increasing frequency we're also finding that to be true! *All of these,* and many more!

### So-Called Solutions

But if that's the problem, then what's the answer? It's *not* in "trial marriages." It's *not* in premarital sex or just living together. That kind of "trial" marriage, as noted by more and more marriage counselors, is more of a burden and a cause for future scars than it could ever be a test! It tests very little, if anything at all! Often it's merely based on expediency. It's based on viewing the partner as an object, a provider of services, a fulfiller of one's personal desires without regard for God or consequences in the lives of many people. It's very often a symptom of a heart growing increasingly rocklike. The answer is *not* in serial marriages, taking one spouse after another, after another, after another, without ever learning anything, without repentance and genuine desire for reconciliation and change. And the answer is *not* in ignoring divorce and saying, "It won't happen in our family. It won't happen to us. We love each other. We've been married for a long, long time."

### Scriptural Answers

"Where's the answer?" you may ask. We need to take a new look at the text and what God teaches us in the Holy Scripture. The question is asked by a few who come up to Jesus, asking, "Can we divorce?" And Jesus responds by saying, "What is God's answer? What does He intend?" The

Bible says, "Have you not read that He who made them from the beginning made them male and female. And He said, 'For this reason a man shall leave his father and mother and be joined to his wife. And so they two shall become one!'"

### What Christ Saw

God desires permanency in marriage. *That's* His desire. *That's* His will. A man, a woman, and God. That's what God wants in marriage. It is the foundation of marriage and family for the whole social order in our country and in every country of the world. But immediately another observation comes up. In our text it says, "But Jesus, even the great teacher, Moses, allowed people to be divorced." It's like saying, "Well, the neighbors did it. Hollywood does it. Can't we?" And perhaps with a sigh on His lips, surely with a look of dismay on His face, Jesus says, "Yes, divorce was allowed, even in the Old Testament times." It still goes on. People still get hurt, and they hurt each other. The issue is not the letter of the law, or even the law of the land, but the issue is our self-centeredness, our pride, and our arrogance. Jesus calls it, "hardness of heart." *Hardness of heart!* And you don't have to be a drug addict in Harlem's ghetto to have a hard heart toward God, or your spouse, or towards parents or children either, for that matter! Nor do you have to be an alcoholic, or poor. Nor do you have to be wealthy! *Hardness of heart* is a disease that is latent in each one of us and we must constantly be on guard against it and see the meaning of our life with God each day. That's what's needed.

### The Root of the Matter

The issue in nearly every marriage-family-divorce problem is a great big "I." This is followed by a huge "ME," and a gigantic "MY," where "God" is often only a word; where He is set on the shelf in life, and where the spouse is viewed as an object of provision or gratification to be used and treated like a tool from a tool box. Where that's the case not even God or His Word will stand a chance of breaking into the heart!

So is divorce wrong? Surely it's wrong. It's *not* what God intends. For God's view of marriage is special. It is sacred and holy and honorable. It is a gift of God for men and women, for all of society. In Heb. 13:4 it says "Let marriage be held in honor among all, and let the marriage bed be undefiled for God will judge the immoral and the adulterous."

### Save a Spouse

By now, some of you may be asking, "Can God forgive a person who divorces his or her spouse?" Well, let me ask, can God forgive a boy who steals? A woman who robs? A man who gossips? A girl who curses? Can God forgive a lying tongue? An income-tax cheater? Did God give His Son, Jesus, to live and to die, to rise from the dead only for moral people? Only for people who are polite and nice? Or clean and well-dressed? Only for people who try hard and who never fail? In Rom. 5 it says, "While we were yet sinners Christ died for us," the godly for the ungodly! That's us! All of us!

What is needed—in our homes, in our families, in our marriages, whenever troubles and problems and tensions begin to arise—what is needed is repentance; a change of heart, a turn-around of life and attitude toward God, a turning towards God. Yes, towards our spouse in marriage! Yes, what is needed is a new view of ourselves as we stand beneath the cross of Jesus, and see Him stretch out His arms for us that we might know the grace of God and receive His power to live a new life. In repentance and in faith in the Lord Jesus Christ, there *is* forgiveness from God. Also, for people who divorce!

As individuals, and as a congregation, we must not forget that. On the other hand, let no one ever take that lightly—the miraculous grace of God's Holy Son, His giving us a new life, His own love, even a new and forgiven record in the eyes of the almighty God! This does *not* mean that we who say we believe in Him dare ever use God's grace as a license for our evil, for our adultery, for misuse of God's great gift of sex and marriage and family life. Tragically, some people have adopted the blasphemous model of the little jingle that goes:

> Free from God's law,
> O happy condition:
> Now I can sin,
> For there is permission.

*That* is hardness of heart! That is a damning disease. It is not Christian freedom.

In Eph. 4:31, St. Paul says, "Do not grieve the Holy Spirit of God, in whom you were sealed for the day of redemption, . . . [but rather] be kind, tenderhearted, forgiving one another, as God in Christ forgave you."

### Save a Home

Can a divorced Christian remarry? Some churches and some pastors take the part of the Bible that we read today word for word, without ever noting its original setting, and some forbid all remarriage. A closer look at the text and the context in which Jesus was speaking shows that in the time of our Lord, a divorced woman was often consigned to a life of prostitution. She often had to sell her body sexually in order to get enough food to stay alive. That's why Jesus, in this historical setting, was so *very hard* on husbands. In effect He is saying, "Do *not* divorce your wife." Some were obviously doing that. And some were doing it *in God's name* claiming that it was okay! The woman, the precious creation of God, was, in effect, being destroyed.

Today men and women, man and wife, can be equally destroyed, and that's why we need to help support, strengthen, and encourage all people in their marriages. We need to do everything possible to urge men and women to be faithful and loyal to *their own* husbands and wives and not tempt them away from each other. And if they ever do separate, or even divorce, we need to do everything we can as friends, as Christian disciples of Jesus, to try to help reconcile and restore what God intended. It is worth years of effort!

### God's Plan

Can a justifiably divorced Christian remarry? It seems plain from the Holy Scriptures that what God wants to know in a situation like that is this: Is there genuine repentance? Is there new learning? Is there a new seeking and discovering of God's forgiveness for sin and God's new direction for life? That's what the living God wants to know. And often only God and the person who is divorced and wants to remarry knows that. *We don't!* On occasion, he or she may share it with a pastor or with another trusted friend. Only later on can the divorced Christian talk openly, but hardly ever painlessly, about what he or she endured in the painful process of divorce. Today, very, very few divorced people are restricted to a life of prostitution for bodily survival. But fewer still find divorce to be utopia or "the wonderful world of happy dreams fulfilled."

I have listened to some on barstools and in the office. Maybe you have, too. What is truly needed is understanding of the God-intended meaning of marriage. What is needed is lots of preparation for it, much more modeling of the listening and forgiving and accepting love of Jesus Christ in our homes and families on the parts of all—husbands and wives and children and all the relatives.

In today's church God Himself has provided a number of helps and resources for people who need encouragement, guidance, and skills in marriage—and prior to it as well. God gives Christian schools, youth and adult Bible studies, Marriage Encounter and similar programs, Effectiveness Training for adults and youth. God gives Christian marriage counselors and doctors and Christian friends. What *we* need to do is to make use of those gifts of God to draw on our Lord's Word, on His presence and strength, His direction for our life: especially in the rough times, when patience begins to grow thin, when understanding becomes weak, when ears begin to turn deaf, and when hearts start to get crusty.

Today, the living God directs us and our spouses, our relatives, our parents, our children, married or unmarried, to our Lord Jesus Christ, to His direction, to His love. He directs us to all of the helpers whom He has provided to bring us His love, His guidance, and His blessing.

May God give to each of us ears to hear, and hearts to believe. May He give us wills to follow Him as we see the greatness of His mercy, His forgiving love for us sinners each day.

### Parallel Scripture Readings

Deuteronomy 24:1-5     Ephesians 5:21-33     Matthew 19:1-12

### Suggested Hymns

Blessed Jesus at Thy Word
Come Unto Me, Ye Weary
Oh, That the Lord Would Guide My Ways

# FAMILIES: WHOLE OR BROKEN

## Marriage and Family

EPHESIANS 5:21-31

It's somewhat dangerous to speak on a touchy subject like *marriage and family* from a pulpit, especially where there is no real opportunity for discussion! It's a dangerous topic because there may be many people present who have many hurts, many wounds, many griefs and sorrows because of marriage or divorce, or broken relationships between spouses or even between parents and children.

It is not the purpose of today's message to rub some old wounds or cause further irritation but rather to take a look at the implications of our faith and our confession of Jesus as our God and Lord. He calls us to live that confession and that faith in the place where it is often the most difficult to be a Christian—at home! They know us so well there!

## When to Be Subject

The text says, "Be subject to one another out of reverence for Christ." At times this text, a very classic one in the Christian view of marriage and family, has been misused by people who see only a few words and interpret and apply them in a sense that St. Paul never intended. Many people take a look at this and see the words, "be subject." Those words have been used as an excuse for many a husband, even supposedly Christian husbands, to treat their wives like pieces of property—something that is owned and possessed, much like what happened in the Old Testament Jewish world. Many arguments have been set forth about the interpretation of this passage in the Scripture from the perspective of the "order of creation" or from the point of a divine chain of command. Many of us have seen the development of that particular syndrome result in the devastation of many homes and families and marriage relationships!

Some Christian people interpret this Scripture about marriage and family as a chain of law and order—only with a homemade emphasis. We see it reflected in some of the so-called "Christian" literature that permeates the market place today—like *The Total Woman,* or other books about the "Christian family." To be sure, there are some valuable pieces of information and insights in some of that material, but more often than not it is stifling the God-given ability, the creativity, and the talents that God has given Christian women and wives. Many a Christian wife has shrunk from personal Christian growth, from service and from responsibility before God and men by saying, "But I'm being subject to my husband. After all, I must do what he wants me to do." In the social realm that's often a cop-out, and in a more extreme form it is pure idolatry, a breaking of the very first commandment of the living God.

### In Reverencing Christ

The text says, "Be subject to one another *out of reverence for Christ.*" That's what the Scripture says. It goes on to talk about the distinctive *role* for husbands and for wives. It does so under that big umbrella of God's grace for all. That umbrella is there because St. Paul spent four of the previous chapters in his letter to the Ephesians, and to us, helping us to understand the meaning of the *grace of God* for all people—young, old, little children, men, women, married, single—whatever our status. Then he comes to a series of specific applications. Now he speaks to wives, and to husbands, and says, "Wives, be subject to your husbands *as to the Lord.*" It probably depends upon the tone of voice with which it is spoken, and the emphasis that is given; but how is the Christian wife to be subject to her husband *"as unto the Lord?"* How do you do that? To be sure, some wives have acted like infants, being influenced by that view of life with God which says, "God is there to give me and I take everything," just like a little infant does from its parents. There are others who see this through the eyes of children, growing through a juvenile stage of their life, where much of the response is learned out of a sense of duty, obligation, fear, or even demand. Sometimes people follow this passage out of fear of condemnation! Most human beings, Christian and non-Christian, male and female, live through those stages of life.

The Biblical view of the call of God in Jesus Christ is that we respond to Him by growing in faith—growing in a new fashion. We respond to *Him* and are subject to *Him*. We submit ourselves to Him out of gratitude and thankfulness—willingly, because of His grace, because of His compassion, because of His kindness, His mercy, and self-sacrificing forgiveness for our many sins!

### Who Died for ALL

The Scripture says, "Wives, be subject to your husbands *as to the Lord."* Our Lord did not come into our world to make men or women or children, or anybody, subject to Him by His divine show of power. He did not come to walk our earth as a dictator. He did not carry a big stick to beat people into line, nor whip them with His tongue when they did not do what He wanted them to do. The Son of God came in the reality of the merciful good news of the Creator for sinners. He came for single people as well as married people; young and old, for wives and husbands, children and parents. He came, as the text says, "to give Himself" for God's church, for God's people! He did it by taking on Himself the just punishment of our sin against the almighty God. He took it on Himself and *gave Himself for us* so that we might know His compassion. That's what He did! He gave us a new life before the Almighty. He came to love us when we had messed up our lives and our homes, our relationships with children, with parents, with our spouse. He came so that we might know the mercy of God in the forgiveness of sins, and that with repentant hearts we might turn to Him and receive His forgiveness; and then share it with one another as He has given it to us! That's the way the Lord came. That's the manner in which a Christian, male or female, responds to husband or wife. That's what reverence is all about!

### To Be Subject with ALL Joy

The Gospel of Jesus Christ is like the warm morning sun, shining through the windows of the sanctuary, shining on the people. That's the way the Gospel of God's Son comes. Because of Him we can risk taking off "our overcoats," our self-preserving shells, the scars and hurts that we sometimes clutch around us so that no one can see our faults, our frailties, or our failings. God comes so that we might walk with Him in reverence, so that we might do that as husband and wife in the marriage relationship.

Jesus Christ is like the warm sun. He is not like the cold north wind that comes and blows and howls and yells and tries to tear off the coat from our back, so that we can again be exposed to the elements around us. No, that's not the way Jesus comes. He does not come like the north wind. Therefore, in marriage, *Christian* husbands and wives are called to "be subject to one another *out of reverence,* "out of honor, out of thanksgiving and gratitude to the Lord who speaks to us of His grace and His mercy! When we think about it, our divine Lord even gave His life on the cross on Calvary. He is the One who promises to be with us day by day. This Lord has even opened wide the gates of *heaven* for husbands and wives and parents and children, for the single *and* for the married! He is the reason we subject ourselves to one another!

In the text, St. Paul goes on to say, "Husbands, love your wives as Christ loved the church and gave Himself up for her, that He might sanctify [the church] having cleansed us by the washing of water with the Word, that He might present the church to Himself in splendor, without spot or wrinkle or any such thing." Did you catch that? God says, *"Men,* you who believe in Me, this is the way you will gain that response, that reverence from your wife. Love as Christ loved the church. That's the way it's done!" You might often say, as I often have, "But how, O Lord? How could we ever begin to do a thing like that when we see the picture of such sacrifice, service, dedication, and willingness? How could we *ever* begin to love as Jesus loved the church? Who could ever do that?" We can't! That's why we need to know where to turn!

### Strength in Him

We need to do what the disciples of Jesus have always done. We can only find that ability, strength, and encouragement to be able to love and to give freely of ourselves as Christian men *as we draw on the strength of our God!* That's where we get it. That's where it comes from. We do not find that help in a pagan world and a pagan society that chiefly causes people to look out for good old number one. We do not find it in an accumulation of things or possessions; or by providing a whole bunch of stuff for our family or our children or our spouses! Not at all!

We find it in the God of the covenant, the God of Abraham, Isaac,

Jacob, Moses, and Joshua, the God who came to our earth in the person of Jesus Christ, the God who freely gave Himself on Calvary's cross so that even those doubting and wayward disciples, like you and me and all of us, might know the meaning of the acceptance of God Himself! As we turn to Him in honest and contrite hearts, in all humility, in confession of our weakness and our failings in our homes and families, in our relationships with our children and our parents and with one another, we hear for ourselves the Word of Life! God says to us again this day, "My son, my daughter—be of good cheer for your sins are forgiven!" We hear Him say, "There is no condemnation for those who are in Christ Jesus." We hear Him say, "I am the Bread of life. He who comes and eats of Me will never hunger, and he who drinks of Me will never thirst."

### Honored in His Association

That word of God's divine grace strengthens us to know the honor and the dignity God has bestowed upon us as men and women, male and female, single or married: And then, with that honor and that dignity before our very eyes we look upon our partners in marriage, our children, our fathers and our mothers, our grandparents and all of those around us, in a new light. As this happens, Christian wives learn what it means when St. Paul says, "Love your husbands *as you would love the Lord.*" As this happens, Christian men will know what it means when God says, "Love your wife *as Jesus Christ loves you* and gave Himself for you" so that you might be a man of God.

So, you, young men, who one day think of marrying a wife, find one whom you can serve, one you can love, one who knows the dignity that she is a child of the living God and will share that with you as a human man.

And you, young women, who think of marrying a husband some day, find one who knows the love of Jesus Christ, who can freely give of himself because he is loved by God, because he possesses the honor and dignity of having his sins forgiven and knows, very personally, that chief blessing in his life! Don't find a partner just because he or she may be attractive or good looking or be well-educated or have a good position or earn a lot of money. Those things are bonuses in life with God. What counts is the *substance of the soul* and the heart and the life. When that is present, love can grow. The New Testament view of marriage is that a man and a woman and the Lord Jesus Christ continually grow together and walk through life together. In that partnership we learn what it means when the Scripture says, "Be subject to one another out of reverence for the Lord Jesus Christ." May God grant that among us in growing fashion.

**Parallel Scripture Readings**

Deuteronomy 6:1-9        John 2:1-11        Luke 10:38-42
Ephesians 5:21—6:4

**Suggested Hymns**

With the Lord Begin Thy Task
In Thee Is Gladness
Oh, Blest the House, Whate'er Befall

# WHAT DOES IT MEAN TO BE BORN AGAIN?

## Dry Bones Alive

EZEKIEL 37:1-14

A pastor received a letter commending his church for sponsoring a unique neighborhood ministry to meet the needs of the community. The writer did not identify with any church or denomination. He simply claimed to be a "born again" Christian. Both inside and outside the local churches, Christians are stepping forth with a new identity. They claim to be "born again," signifying a radical change in their lives resulting in joy and peace and zeal for the Lord.

Indeed, the claim to new life and vitality in the church is like a breath of fresh air. Some observers see the church in America going the way of Christianity in England and Europe where less than 10 percent of the population attends worship services. If as many as 40 percent of the American people attend church on Sunday, much is still to be desired. The portion of our population only nominally attached to a local church is staggering. The collective number of persons in the church who are only remotely related to the preaching of the Word suggests some points of comparison to Ezekiel's vision of the valley of dry bones.

### I. Dry Bones—A Condition of Man
#### A. Nature of the Condition

Ezekiel, captive with thousands of his countrymen, was exiled to Babylon. He was one of the early exiles, deported with King Jehoiakim. While in Babylon, God called him to prophesy. In the first half of his prophecy, Ezekiel reflects on the fall of Jerusalem and the miseries of his fellow exiles. He explains the plight of the captive, homesick people of Judah as God's visitation of judgment upon their lack of repentance. In captivity the complaint (Ezek. 18: 25, 29) went up from the people, "The way of the Lord is not equal [not just]!" But the prophet replied, it was their ways that were unequal or unjust.

In the latter half of the Book of Ezekiel, in chapter 37, the prophet foretells God's future restoration of His people who had been spiritually bankrupt, even lifeless. That restoration was vividly described in a vision for Ezekiel. In this vision, the prophet was transported to a hot desert valley of that arid country of Babylon. Presumably there had been a great conflict between armies of two major powers in that valley. Imagine what Ezekiel saw, a battlefield where thousands of the dead lay strewn over the desert sands. Here a chariot wheel and there a sword protruding from the sand, and a helmet resting where it rolled from its fallen head, its glorious plume now faded. But one hardly noticed these remnants of war for all the bones and skeletal shapes of skulls and rib cages and limbs scattered about.

"The entire plain was white with the chronic leprosy of death. And it was the chill of old death, death grown grey and sere, death itself turned dead. . . . It was death long settled down into dismal possession, death established, privileged, throned, and secure."[1] Ezekiel was the only living man walking in this valley of bones. It was eerie. And what was the meaning of it? "Dry bones, exceeding many and exceeding dry. The slain. All hope lost. We are clean cut off. The grave." Against this ghastly background, God raises this question for the prophet (Ezek. 37:3), "Son of Man, can these bones live?"

### B. Spiritual Counterpart to the Condition

Ezekiel's vision is only a mirror of the decay, despair, and spiritual death we observe in our society, in the church, and in our personal lives. The symptoms are everywhere. Today we have superior means of communication, but we have less and less of important and helpful things to say. The same electronics employed to keep a man alive, setting a pacer alongside his heart in the chest cavity, are also employed in underhanded ways to effect thievery and other intrusions on privacy and individual freedom. We are a nation sometimes more careful to protect animal life than to safeguard human beings. Why is the unborn child exempted from the concern and outrage expressed by some environmentalists? A woman who will brake for animals on the highway may be driving to an abortion clinic to be done with an unwanted child. It is sickness in the soul. It is death. Dry bones.

The decay is part of us, and we are part of the decay. We lay up for ourselves prosperity, yet few of us are seeking to turn the good of the land into profit for anyone except ourselves. We pour prime energies into sports and clubs and vacations and parties and entertainment. Still we are empty within. The soul goes begging. It is unfulfilled. Our churches are filled with persons who lead two lives. They profess allegiance to the true God, but they have not discovered ways to follow through and serve God. So many neighbors near and distant, because of our ofttimes casual contacts, are not even remembered long enough to recognize or help them with their needs. We speak or sing a few lines of the liturgy, a few hymn verses, but the heart is distant from God. Many are hiding in the transcepts, as it were, hoping not to be discovered, hoping that no one will ask us to look alive as a true Christian who serves for no other reason than to honor Christ the Lord.

## II. Dry Bones—Challenge to God
### A. Only God Is Interested

Our world, our church, and our personal lives are compared to a valley of dry bones. Who can change this condition? The question falls upon mute and helpless humanity. All that we are able to say is, "All hope is lost." Can the dead bring life to the dead? "We are cut off. We are in our graves" (Ezek. 37:11).

Return to our Scripture text. The prophecy of Ezekiel now yields a divine word of grace. Praise the Lord! In the midst of this valley of dry bones, God (v. 3) asks, "Son of Man, can these bones live?" That is the question. There is only one answer, the answer of Ezekiel, "O Lord God, thou knowest." That is what God wants us to say with respect to our world, conditions in the church, and our personal lives. For, in saying, "Thou knowest!" we begin to taste the sweetness of hope and victory because God does know. He says, "O dry bones, hear the Word of the Lord." Then says the Lord God to those bones, "Behold I will cause breath to enter you, and you shall live!" (v. 4). Thou knowest, O Lord God, that it can happen. These bones, even these dry bones can live!

### B. Only God Is Adequate for the Challenge

Who else would bother with dry bones except God? The sin and the evil and the disappointment and despair of depraved humanity on every front spell a losing battle, yes, a battle that has been lost. Who can see in the death and defeat of dry bones a vision of life except, perhaps, God Himself? But, by the power of His Spirit, God can visualize, not only flesh and sinew and clothing of skin upon those dry bones, He can also give His own pulsating life. "I will open your graves and raise you from your graves" (v. 12). "Behold, I will cause breath to enter into you, and ye shall live!" (v. 5). Decisively, it is God and God alone, the breath of God, His Holy Spirit, that can turn death to life.

### C. God Meets the Challenge with New Life

When God gives life and breath, it is for real, and it is not to be mistaken or confused with apparent dressing up of the dry bones. No imitations, God gives real life! Learn from the prophet Ezekiel. He writes, ". . . and as I prophesied, there was a voice, and behold a shaking, and the bones came together, bone to his bone. And when I beheld, lo, the sinews and the flesh came up upon the bones, and the skin covered them above; but there was no breath in them" (v. 7, 8). What? "There was no breath in them!" The prophet is given a vision of dry bones having all the dressing of sinews and flesh, the appearance of health and vitality, but the condition is still death, still nothing more than dry bones. The renewal and revival is not yet complete. God must yet give the life of His Spirit, or else nothing can really live.

A nation may advance to a refined appearance of civilization. It may clean up its cities, extend education to all, inaugurate drastic social reform, raise the standard of living and elevate the quality of life for its citizens, but without the breath of the Spirit of God in its national heart, the life He brings will be missing. And all else is little more than dressing for dry bones. Because the Spirit of God and the life He brings is lacking in parts of the church, we may have a congregation, but the fellowship can hardly be the communion of saints. We have an assembly, but hardly an army for God. We may be just a crowd. We cannot be the family of the living God except the Spirit bring to us His breath and life.

Raise a child in Sunday school and Christian day school, send him to Lutheran High School and a Christian college or seminary, put him in office as a pastor or teacher, and even all of this may be so much external dressing, so much sinew and flesh. Underneath are the dry bones and death except that man be filled with God's life and power. Where there is no life of God's Spirit, there is only death and dry bones. You have seen precision wax statues of human beings, perfect models of the original person such as those displayed in the Wax Museum in Washington, D. C. The similarity to the real person is so close that there is only one way to tell the difference when the subject is a contemporary individual. You could stand this person next to the wax statue and not be able to tell the difference except by one single criterion. "Which one is breathing?" Are you breathing? Are you a breathing, living Christian? Except we breathe with the breath of God's Spirit, all the apparent signs of life and vitality are only living death. The God who created man not only of sinews and flesh and skin, but breathed into his nostrils the breath of life, must now take this fallen and sinful man and breathe again into His soul the life-giving breath of His Spirit.

### III. Dry Bones—New Life
#### A. The Spirit Gives Life

And it happens! Yes, it does happen. Ezekiel brings the word of the Lord to the broken and hopeless captives. The Lord says, "And I will put my Spirit within you, and you shall live, and I will place you in your own land; then you shall know that I, the Lord, have spoken, and I have done it, says the Lord" (Ezek. 37:14). And you ask, how does God breathe life into His people today? That is very clear. Jesus said, "When the Spirit of truth comes, He will guide you into all truth; for He will not speak on His own authority, but whatever He hears He will speak. . . . He will glorify Me, for He will take what is Mine and declare it unto you. All that the Father has is Mine; therefore, I said that He will take what is Mine and declare it unto you" (John 16:13-15).

This means that the Holy Spirit has no other program for giving life and power except by the agent of Jesus Christ and His heavenly Father. It was the Father's love that sent the Son to the cross as our Redeemer. The Son laid down His life, taking our sins away. Whoever sees and believes the Son shall have life! The Holy Spirit breathes nothing new of himself, but only what Jesus Christ has taught and accomplished via His birth, His suffering and death, and His resurrection. Beginning at our baptism and throughout our lives under the Gospel in Word and Sacrament, the Spirit of God is drawing us into the death of Christ, where, in the same motion of death to sin, life through Jesus Christ is given and sealed by the Spirit of God. The world needs this renewal, the church needs it, and we as individuals need the same ongoing work of the Spirit giving life and power through Jesus Christ.

### B. The Life of Those Who Live in Christ

Life given by the Spirit is not power to continue as usual in the old sinful and selfish ways. No, life given by the Spirit of God is a life under the lordship of Christ. That was hinted already in Ezekiel's prophecy (v. 13) which reads, "I will . . . put breath in you; and you shall live; and you shall know that I am the Lord!" Synonymous with being alive is to know that God is the Lord. No man has lived until he lives for a goal higher than himself. No man really lives until he lives for Christ. The Spirit bids the response from the depths of your heart, confessing, "Jesus Christ is Lord!" This is life, and it signifies bringing down all the other lords in your life that Christ may in all things be supreme.

The lordship of Christ was the confession of the early church. "If thou shalt confess with thy mouth the Lord Jesus, and shalt believe in thine heart that God hath raised Him from the dead, thou shalt be saved"(Rom. 10: 9). When a Jewish convert to Christianity in the first century said, "Jesus is Lord," he meant that Jesus was God; and when a Gentile believer said, "Jesus is Lord," he meant that Caesar was no longer his god. Jesus Christ was his God. In the New Testament, it is never "Christ and . . ." because one never needs to add anything to Jesus. He is Alpha and Omega, and the entire alphabet between. He is everything. So, it is, "Christ or . . . the world," "Christ or . . . Satan," "Christ or . . . Caesar." Early Christianity demanded a clean break with the world, the sinful flesh, and the devil. Life in Christ by the Spirit of God could not tolerate spiritual death. Christian life and vitality by the Spirit exclude and replace the dominion of sin and decay and depravity.

### God's Spirit Breathes Life

The Spirit of God breathes life! The Spirit pleads with you to receive Jesus Christ the crucified and powerful Savior to be Lord of your life today. A host of people will say that they accept Christ in order to miss hell and reach heaven. They want to go the long road with Christ into eternity and glory, but on the short road here in time, they have little patience to live under Christ as their Lord. But the life given by the Spirit of God is life under the lordship of Jesus Christ.

Have you observed that the word, "Savior," occurs only 24 times in the New Testament, while the term, "Lord," is found 433 times? To be a "born again" Christian is to enjoy new life and vitality. It is to discover new direction and purpose and meaning in your daily life. What this means is that the Spirit of God places you under the lordship of Him who lived and died for you and rose again as the risen Lord.

Is Jesus your Lord? Is He Lord of your thoughts, your tongue, your temperament, and your temper? Is He Lord of your spare time, your life's plans, your work, your dollars and investments, your church life, your recreation? Is Jesus the Lord of your home? His lordship extends over everything from eating and drinking to the most formidable challenges we face in life. Living under this Lord is not bondage. It is life and freedom. The Spirit of God brings us to this freedom under the lordship of Christ.

And, ". . . where the Spirit of the Lord is, there is liberty" (2 Cor. 3:17). There is life! The Spirit and you and Jesus Christ, Savior and Lord: "And the breath came into them, and they lived, and stood upon their feet, an exceedingly great host!" (v. 10). The world, the church, you and I, dry bones come alive!

### Parallel Scripture Readings

Ezekiel 36:22-28                          Acts 10:42-48

### Suggested Hymns

From All That Dwell Below the Skies
Come, Holy Ghost in Love
Beautiful Savior

# WHAT DOES IT MEAN TO BE BORN AGAIN?

## You Must Be Born Again

JOHN 3:1-15

Nicodemus and Jesus talked late into the night. Had the subject been politics or economics, their conversation would not prevail to enlighten us today. But, here we are, eavesdropping, as it were, on a conversation between Jesus and a man of influence from the Sanhedrin. From that discussion, St. John reports one of Jesus' most important sayings, "Except a man be born again, he cannot see the kingdom of God" (v. 3).

Is there a pulpit anywhere in the land where this saying of Jesus about regeneration, new spiritual birth, has not been proclaimed with great intensity? "You must be born again!" The 18th-century English divine, George Whitefield, preached 300 times on this text, the Gospel of St. John, chapter 3, verse 7. Yes, 300 sermons, the equivalent of six years of preaching in our church, and all those messages arising from this word of Jesus with Nicodemus that night, "You must be born again!"

### I. People
#### A. Empty

Some of us are so saturated with personal testimonials that it seems we have sat through all 300 of Whitefield's sermons. It is all you hear today, one celebrity after another attesting to their new life, telling the world what it means to be a "born again" Christian. If it is not Charles Colson, it is Keith Miller. Or, it is Terry Bradshaw of the Pittsburgh Steelers or some member of the Dallas Cowboys football team or coaching staff. Saturated as we are and weary as we may be, hearing countless testimonials, we are still curious to ask, what has happened to these people? Is there something to this "born again" life? Is it for me?

Nicodemus was a leader of the Jewish Sanhedrin. He rose to heights of fame and respectability. He was a prominent man. Probably he was financially secure. Yet, he seeks Jesus for private counsel in the night. What burdens weighed heavy on this man's heart? Was Nicodemus like some people who have everything and yet feel empty inside as if they had nothing? Whitefield could preach those 300 sermons from this text about Nicodemus and Jesus because the world then and also the churches now are filled with people who are searching for ultimate meanings and reasons to live.

### B. Spiritually Hungry

Many persons awaken late in life to a distinctive spiritual hunger. They were properly educated, enjoyed success in their profession or business, and discovered fulfillment in their marriage and family. Then, in the midst of their middle years, they realize that a vital part of their life has been sorely neglected. And perhaps they have conveniently avoided giving attention to spiritual needs for many years. When they become sensitive to these needs and witness how a man like Nicodemus was drawn to Jesus because of the Savior's compelling words and works, they, too, cannot stay away. They must meet with Jesus also. For some 40 years they may have been on the run, keeping a safe distance from God. Now, like Nicodemus they are ready to "seek the Lord where He may be found" (Is. 55:6).

### C. Unfulfilled

When Charles Colson left government service after the 1972 presidential election and went back to private law practice, he visited a former client, Tom Phillips. A successful executive, Mr. Phillips had become president of Raytheon Company, an electronics manufacturer and the largest employer in New England. Colson noticed something different about his former client. Phillips explained, "Yes, I have accepted Jesus Christ. I have committed my life to Him, and it has been the most marvelous experience of my whole life. . . . I'd like to tell the whole story some day. . . . I had gotten to the point where I didn't think my life was worth anything. Now everything has changed—attitude, values, the whole bit." Remembering that conversation, Colson recalls, "Phillips was boggling my mind. Life isn't worth anything, he says, when you're president of the biggest company in the state, have a beautiful home, a Mercedes, a great family, probably a quarter-million-a-year salary?"

Whatever your reaction may be to Watergate and men like Charles Colson, one has to be impressed by the affect which Tom Phillips and his Christian witness had on the former presidential aid. Ultimately, Colson professed his faith in Jesus Christ. Both Phillips and Colson were men like Nicodemus who came to Christ later in life. Each of them had been nominally members of a church. Colson was Episcopalian. Phillips had been Congregational. But church membership meant little to these men until later in life when they confronted the appeal in Jesus' words, "You must be born again!" Those words struck a responsive chord in their hearts just as the call to regeneration had fulfilled a need in the life of Nicodemus.

## II. Power
### A. Apart from Man

What does all of this mean? Is there a formula for possessing the new and exciting life of a "born again" Christian? Sometimes we oversimplify the matter, or perhaps we make it more complex by suggesting that a man like Nicodemus only had to turn on when it came to religion. We may expect that Jesus would have counseled Nicodemus to make his decision, pray about it, and commit himself to the Lord. Religion, after all, is mostly what you make it to be. All we have to do is take a few steps in God's direction, get our thinking straightened out, turn our lives in the direction of the Lord, and everything will be different. We stand to have the same peace and joy in our hearts, the same fulfillment that Phillips and Colson and others have discovered. A few minor adjustments in thinking and living, and the "born again" style will be ours to enjoy. Thus, it is often surmised.

If this is a typical formula for moving into the new life of the Spirit, we may be surprised to discover a pattern quite distinctive as Jesus spoke about conversion and regeneration in His conversation with Nicodemus. Jesus literally stunned this fine man. Nicodemus was perhaps looking for some concrete steps to take in the direction of his conversion. But Jesus gave Nicodemus no instructions. There was nothing for him to do. Jesus did not even ask Nicodemus to turn his life over to God. He did not ask him to do a thing. And the implication is clear. There is nothing that we can do in order to come to a new life and experience all that it means to be a "born again" Christian. We do not come to that radical change in our lives by prompting or coaxing ourselves to be the Christian we want ourselves to become. Jesus did not say, you decide, you yield, or give yourself to the Lord. Rather, He started at the beginning—before there is even a chance for us to entertain the notion of giving ourselves back to God. To Nicodemus, a man with a sterling reputation, a man with much learning and wisdom, a religious man, Jesus addressed those startling words, "Except a man be born again, he cannot see the kingdom of God!"

### B. Agent—the Holy Spirit

Nicodemus immediately replied (v. 4), "How can a man be born when he is old? Can he enter a second time into his mother's womb and be born?" Jesus disclaimed the literal sense of physical rebirth, but He did employ this dramatic analogy of birth and life to show how helpless we are to effect new spiritual life. He wanted to convince Nicodemus that becoming a "born again" Christian was up to an agent elsewhere than in himself, namely, the Spirit of God.

Consider the analogy for a moment. You may know the day on the calendar when you celebrate your birthday. But, can you remember the time you were born? What were the newspaper headlines that day? And think about five years before that day. Were you even thought about by anyone? Did you exist in any manner that can be explained except perhaps in the foreknowledge of God? It was, then, God's plan and the parenting of father and mother which served as agents to bring you to life in this world on the day of your birth quite apart from any decisions or actions on your part.

And we are equally helpless to bound into the kingdom of God or soar to new spiritual heights by our own decisions and action. We must be born into that new life, and the agent for this spiritual rebirth is the Holy Spirit. Yes, we are endowed with a mind and power of the will. We make decisions. But, are we able to decide to become alive, to be "born again"? Dr. Luther reminded us long ago how impossible it is for our sinful nature to generate its own new birth. His explanation to the Third Article of the Apostles' Creed begins, "I cannot by my own reason or strength believe in Jesus Christ, my Lord, or come to Him; but the Holy Ghost has called me by the Gospel."

The Scriptures will not debate with Dr. Carl Jung on this point when the great psychologist said, "All the old, primitive sins are not dead but are crouching in the dark corners of our modern hearts." God is direct and His judgment is severe when He renders His divine estimate of our sinful nature. According to His Word, man is "the enemy of God" (Rom. 5:10).

He is "alienated from the life of God" (Eph. 4:18); and he is "guilty before God" (Rom. 3:19), and "under the wrath of God" (John 3:36). Our nature, call it our ego, our person, together with our pride, comprise what the Bible calls the sinful flesh which cannot inherit or prepare itself to be an heir of the kingdom of God. This sinful nature is dead in trespasses and sins (Eph. 2:1; 1 Cor. 15:50). Jesus says, "Nicodemus, you are religious, you are well informed about religion, you are prominent and powerful in the eyes of men. But, unless you are born again, you cannot see the kingdom of God!'

### C. The Means, Holy Baptism

And who is stepping out ahead of Nicodemus? No one may boast of his own works or his own walk with the Lord or his own track into a new relationship with God. Most of the testimonials we hear ultimately proclaim that the new birth is effected by God through grace. Whatever we may think contributes to conversion or new life must be set aside as St. Paul exclaimed, "But whatever gain I had, I counted as loss for the sake of Christ" (Phil. 3:7). If you are following the thoughts expressed by our Lord to Nicodemus, you are probably ready to sigh and conclude that becoming a Christian and remaining a Christian and growing to be a more lively and dedicated Christian is nothing short of a miracle.

And that conclusion is right on, so to speak. Indeed, spiritual rebirth or regeneration is a miracle effected by "water and the Spirit," says Jesus (v. 5). He is speaking about God's all important agent for creating this new life. It is out of our hands, it is all God's action, by "water and the Spirit." And Jesus is speaking about Holy Baptism, that gracious water of regeneration and renewal of the Holy Ghost, the cleansing which washes away sins as we are baptized into Christ Jesus. In Baptism the Holy Spirit begets a new life which you never had before you were brought to the Gospel. You do not interrupt the normal course of living to claim this new life. You do not leave home. You need not embark upon some bizarre retreat isolated from your day-to-day responsibilities. You go to work as usual. All these circumstances remain the same, but *you are not the same!* Baptized into Christ, you have put on Christ. You put on His righteousness, His victory, His life, and ultimately you will put on His glory (Gal. 3:26-27).

## III. Program
### A. Directed by the Spirit

Our minds stretch and reach out to grasp and understand. If only we were able to comprehend more perfectly how the Spirit awakens in us new life! But this miracle is beyond the reach of the most astute minds. Jesus compares the movements of the Holy Spirit to the elusive wind. Even modern meteorology is baffled by the complex phenomena that are components of the wind. "The wind"—Christ's country-clean symbol of God's Spirit—"blows where it wills" (v. 8). How the wind blows, from whence it comes, and where it goes, no one really knows. ". . . so it is with every one who is born of the Spirit" (v. 8b).

But you do see trees bending and branches waving and leaves moving. It is the wind. You do feel the breeze. And mystery that conversion is, there are signs of the Spirit's working, begetting new life. There are people from whom we least expected to hear a Christian testimony, people saying that the greatest thing that happened to them was when they were born again or born by power from above. As a result they know Jesus Christ and confess Him as their Savior and Lord. They have become new-born children of God (John 1:12-13).

And their story is repeated throughout history. There was the rich and popular young Italian youth, Giovanni. At a party his friends crowned him, "King of Revelers." But suddenly this young man voluntarily left the party. Later his friends found him to be a serious person whom Christ claimed by His Spirit. This youth, Giovanni Francesco Bernardone, became the gentle and compassionate man of God known in history as Francis of Assisi.

Another young man of the 20th century, a student leader at Oxford, was a clever and cynical young agnostic. His chief joy was casting barbs at Christians and the Christian faith. This brilliant youth had a large following among the students at Oxford. But the Lord was on his trail. Twist and turn as he would, he realized that there was ultimately no escape. The crisis came one night in Magdalen College. In his own bedroom he knelt in prayer and made his commitment to Christ. His name? C. S. Lewis, one of the most able defenders of Christianity in Britain.

### B. The New Life Takes New Direction

What does it mean to be a person like C. S. Lewis or St. Francis? What does it mean to be a "born again" Christian? So many answers are given in response to that question. For some persons it means a closer walk with the Lord, a life conformed to the Biblical record of Jesus' way of life. Others experience a new hunger for the teachings of the Bible and a new capacity to love and forgive as Christ has loved and forgiven us. Some Christians enjoy a rich prayer life and exhibit new spiritual gifts. The experiences and the testimonials are many, but there are two unmistakable marks of this life. The "born again" Christian shuns all sin, and he is drawn to Christ who was lifted to the cross as our Redeemer. That is what the Lord is speaking about in the remaining verses of this third chapter of John's Gospel. Moses raised the serpent in the wilderness to deliver the people from the sickness and death caused by the bite of the poisonous reptiles. So, Christ was raised on the cross to draw all men to Himself that He might deliver them from the power of sin in their lives. A "born again" Christian looks to Christ, lives by the power of Christ, and also lives for Christ. And at all times he shuns the sinner's ways (John 3:14 f.; 1 John 3:4-12).

### By Water and the Spirit

May we call ourselves "born again" Christians? Certainly, we may claim that identity as long as we live each day in the power of God by "water and the Spirit." Some of the most meaningful moments in this church have been the times when we administered Holy Baptism. You were baptized! And, baptized into Christ Jesus, you were made a new person with new life. Then, begin each day on the high note of your baptism, and go on to live in Christ Jesus. Read your Scriptures, pray, walk with the Lord, and live the victory! By "water and the Spirit" you are a "born again" Christian. Praise God!

### Parallel Scripture Readings

Titus 3:4-8          Romans 6:1-8       John 15:1-9

### Suggested Hymns

God Loved the World
Jesus, Thy Blood and Righteousness
Just as I Am, Without One Plea

# WHAT DOES IT MEAN TO BE BORN AGAIN?

## Reborn Citizens of Heaven

PHILIPPIANS 3:17—4:1

A mother was helping her son put on his coat and hat. He was going to a birthday party. She did not say, "Be good!" or "Behave yourself!" The last words of this wise mother were, "Son, remember who you are!"

"Remember!" It was the apostle's word to Christians at Philippi. Remember, because you are not only citizens of Rome and residents of Macedonia, you are not only shopkeepers and businessmen and merchants and housewives and boys and girls. You are citizens of heaven. Remember who you are!

A decal in a rear car window read, "I am a china painter." Were you aware that there is a fraternity of persons who paint china and ceramics? I was surprised that china painters have such fierce pride to tell the world about their skill. The thought occurred, "Why not a decal for car windows to tell the world, we are God's people?" At a banquet for Christian leaders, someone made the comment, the Lord has no "secret agents" in His organization. You are a "born again" Christian. How open are you about your identity as a Christian? Living day to day at home or in the world, is it obvious to those around you that you are a person who seeks those things which are above? Do you walk in this world as a Christian pilgrim? Consider this morning:

### The Christian Is a Citizen of Heaven
#### I. Destiny

In a certain sense, all mankind is on a venture which some call a pilgrimage. Christians are moving through life in much the same way, only they are going somewhere. They have a destiny. And the prospect of that eternal life affects the quality of living while we are on the journey. The Israelites in the wilderness seemed to travel and get nowhere. They keenly felt a sense of futility many times. Yet, all the while they were citizens of the Promised Land. They were God's people in the wilderness, and the Land which God had promised was already their land. They traveled, but they were never nomads, with no place to call home. They belonged to a land. All the while they journeyed somewhat helplessly and aimlessly, they had a home. At last God made good His promise. They arrived home beyond Jordan in the good land.

Regenerated by the Holy Spirit through Baptism into Christ Jesus, we were set on a journey toward a glorious inheritance. "Born again" Christians are pilgrims, even foreigners in this present age. Buried with Christ by Baptism, we are also raised with Him to a quality of life that is characteristically, "other worldly." Someone said, we are called to holiness. With Christ, we are raised above the passions, fears, and bondage of this sinful age to set our hearts on things which are above. "For here have we no continuing city, but we seek one which is to come" (Heb. 13:14). We are registered. Our names are written in the Book of Life. We are on

God's rolls. We have our citizenship in heaven as men free from the bonds of sin and death and mortality.

About much of life you will ask, was I born for this? Ask that question about your baptism. Yes, you were born again in Christ for higher things. At the Lord's Table we are drawn away to the cross and God's peace and forgiveness of sins and the life that has an eternal destiny. For this you were indeed, "born again." Life now has stakes that are eternal with the living God and the saints in glory. Take a little time each day, free your mind from business, taxes, and eletions. Consider your citizenship in heaven. You will become aware of a growing force to attach your heart to realities of the other world. And you will want to set your affection on things above and spend your life's energies and resources in the direction where neither moth nor rust corrupt.

### II. Allegiance

This new citizenship to which we were born in our baptism calls for a loyalty even more intense than the fraternalism of those diehard china painters mentioned a moment ago. Our heavenly citizenship prevails above everything else in this life. Dr. Albert Schweitzer sensed that peculiar magnetism of citizenship above when he left behind three careers in theology, medicine, and music to become a jungle doctor at Lambarene deep in remotest Africa. It was this heavenly citizenship, about which St. Paul writes, that came to the fore in Albert Schweitzer and in the lives of all the great men and women of faith. Their primary loyalty was Jesus Christ. For Christ and Christ alone was the Lord.

A long stretch of Massachusetts Avenue in Washington, D. C. is known as embassy row where many foreign diplomats live and work in homes away from home. While they reside in our nation's capitol, they obey the laws of our land, eat meals in our restaurants, sent their children to American schools, and watch major network TV. But, these diplomats are first and foremost loyal citizens of another land. The flag flown outside a particular embassy symbolizes that allegiance and expresses the hope that one day when their work is complete they may return to their beloved homeland.

How well do you fly the flag as a Christian? Do you realize that you and your family as Christians are an embassy or a colony in this world? Are you solid citizens of heaven? The Philippians understood St. Paul clearly. The city of Philippi was a colony of Rome. And Rome's colonies began as military outposts or garrisons. Later they became settlements for veterans of the Roman army and their households. The chief characteristic of these colonies was that, wherever they were founded, they remained fragments of Rome itself. The people wore Roman dress, observed Roman customs, and spoke the Latin language of Rome. The magistrates had Roman titles, dispensed Roman justice and carried out the same civil ceremonies conducted in Rome. Though residents of a foreign city, the people never forgot their primary allegiance to Rome. Their citizenship in Rome was counted as one of the highest privileges any man in the ancient world could possess.

### III. Privilege

Do we cherish the high privilege of our citizenship in heaven? When someone asked Sir James Simpson, who discovered the use of chloroform as an anesthetic, to name the greatest discovery he had ever made, Simpson replied, "The greatest discovery I ever made was that I was a great sinner and Jesus Christ a wonderful Savior." Born again Christians have always been deeply touched by the privilege of citizenship through Christ. The Lord's choice and favor and His call have meant more to Christians than the highest honors the world may bestow. The Lord's Table is more precious than the most distinguished table in the land. Belonging to Christ's church has been a greater privilege than belonging to any school, university, club, or fraternity, because in Christ we are "fellow citizens with the saints," members of that most illustrious company which includes the most admired men and women of the past 19 centuries.

### IV. Security

A special privilege, this grand citizenship in heaven also affords security. When the Roman officer in Jerusalem gave orders to have St. Paul flogged, the apostle stopped him by asking (Acts 22:25), "Is it lawful for you to scourge a man who is a Roman citizen?" The tribune stared at him in disbelief. "I bought this citizenship for a large sum," the tribune boasted with the pride of one who has arrived socially. With the pride of blue blood Paul retorted, "But I was born a citizen!" Immediately Paul was accorded respect and care from the soldiers. What security attended a man like Paul, who, in every city of the ancient world always carried a Roman passport! Wherever he traveled, the Roman citizen was backed by the highest civil power in the world.

Our citizenship in heaven may not guarantee security in the civil realm, but it offers spiritual security in a world sorely affected by the power of evil. Citizenship in heaven affords inner stability and peace; the latter is sorely needed as an alterantive to our hedonistic life-style, which betrays itself as shallow and meaningless when the chips are really down. This brand of security is the apostle's request for the Philippians in the face of those whom he openly and bluntly marks as ". . . enemies of the cross of Christ, whose end is utter destruction, whose god is their belly and that which they esteem to be their glory is their shame, who regard the things upon the earth" (v. 19, Wuest's translations).

Who were these radicals disturbing the church with their earthly life-style? Why were they running counter to the heavenly citizenship of the born-again Christian? Were they perhaps professed Christian Greeks, Epicureans, who brought with them strains of influence from a Greek school of thought that wanted complete satisfaction of the physical appetites as the highest aim of man? There is a current philosophy popularized and practiced much more widely than the distribution of the magazine from which it derives its title. It relies on the assumption that man's needs *en toto* may be fulfilled by giving one's entire attention to earthly things. Advertised on major TV networks, the magazine promises about everything: entertainment, reviews of movies and books, news, sports coverage, interviews with well-known personalities, travel, fashions, and beautiful women. This is the tabloid representation of the life supposedly complete and fulfilled by things earthly.

One only has to walk through a hospital ward or emergency room or court room or cell block to see how lacking, how insecure such a philosophy of life leaves the soul. But our citizenship is in heaven, furnishing us fulfillment of crucial needs, transforming life to be lived not singularly for the present pleasure of man, but directed to the glory of God. It is life redeemed by Christ and sanctified for serving and sacrifice versus attaining selfish enjoyment and pleasure. It is life given to productivity and selfless concern for others versus eating and drinking and living carelessly. It is life that knows right and wrong versus life without either constraint or restraint. It is life fixed on things that are above.

### V. Images

No matter how popular and forceful is the other, alien playboy philosophy and life-style, our citizenship is in heaven. And so we live. So we walk, distinctively, our minds set on things above. There is an old saying, "When in Rome, do as the Romans do!" But, a true citizen of Rome also carried himself as a Roman whether he resided in Ephesus or Jerusalem or Alexandria. And it is the character of heaven's citizens to always walk as citizens of heaven.

Unusual? Different? Odd? Perhaps, but a life-style consistent with one's citizenship has always challenged men to noble behavior. Did you read about the man who entered a hut of a British officer in Africa and saw his friend sitting at a perfectly set table and clad in a formal dinner jacket? The visitor said, "Man, are you crazy? Dressing for dinner out here in the bush?" "No," replied the officer. "I dress for dinner once a week. I have to. I belong to the British Empire, and my customs and standards are not those of the bush country." What kind of moral and spiritual bush country has become our habitat? What kind of jungle? "Don't go native!" St. Paul admonishes Christian citizens. Resist the pressure of your environment. It may descend upon you with a fury. But, remember, your commonwealth, your citizenship is above.

How can we be strong? How can we be solid citizens of heaven this side of heaven in a world given to pursuit of earthly things? St. Paul suggests that we find an exemplary person, some noble Christian stronger and more valiant than ourselves and imitate that example. How good it is for us to keep our eyes fixed on noble men and women of the faith! "Become imitators of me, brethren." says Paul (v. 17). The apostles and saints and heroes of faith, mark their courage, their mastery, their victory. Mark how their citizenship in heaven commanded their highest allegiance.

There must have been something rare about the very "walk" of this man, St. Paul. He never apologized for the Savior. He was never ashamed of the Gospel. He was totally committed to Christ. And his very "walk" with the Lord must have been magnificent. They say that men whose calling makes them pass their days and live their lives in the vast aisles and beneath the spacious domes and rotundas of the great cathedrals instinctively acquire a certain stateliness which gives them kinship to the spirit that pervades those sacred halls and sanctuaries. If you want to walk big as a Christian, walk alongside a big Christian. Discover such a person in the church, a leader, a teacher, a theologian, or pastor. Or that person may be a grandmother and her well-read Bible and childlike faith. Discover some person, some noble Christian, who has lived in the presence of the Lord. Imitate that person's Christian walk and heavenly citizenship.

### VI. Hope

That Christian walk ultimately carries us beyond this world for we await a Savior, the Lord Jesus Christ (v. 20b). In the ancient world Roman citizenship gave a man the hope that some day he might visit Rome and see the Eternal City, walk through the Forum and stand before Caesar's palace, perhaps to get a glimpse of Caesar himself. And our citizenship in heaven gives the hope that we, who have not seen Christ, but only served Him, may at last meet the Lord face to face.

Then, all things will be new. And our bodies, not "vile" as the Authorized Version translates, not despicable, but the body that is humiliated in our lowly state, the body which is so often the point of contact with so much that is vanity and evil in our world, the body whose appetites conjur up temptation, these bodies so often hindrances rather than helps to Christian living, bodies which bear the marks of the toll of sin, these very bodies shall rise from their dust and shall be changed in a moment like unto the Lord's body, like Him standing victorious before the open grave, like the body of Jesus on the mount when He was about to ascend into heaven, like His glorious body.

### Glory

O the glory that shall be revealed in us that day! We cannot even imagine its grandeur and beauty, but it shall envelope and encompass our very bodies. Until then, let us live gloriously, our sights fixed on Jesus, looking to Him who is the author and finisher of our faith. And let us walk as becomes the saints of God, living by the faithful examples of Christian heroes past and present, abiding for a time as residents of this age, but living as citizens of heaven. To this life and glory we were born by the Spirit of the living and eternal God!

### Parallel Scripture Readings

Colossians 3:1-17                          Matthew 5:17-27

### Suggested Hymns

Jesus Christ, My Pride and Glory
Renew Me, O Eternal Light
Savior, Again to Thy Dear Name We Raise

# WOMEN OF THE BIBLE

*The Adulteress*

## Forgiveness Instead of Stones

JOHN 8:1-11


Can you imagine the pious Pharisees and the scholarly Scribes dragging a woman to Jesus, whom, they said, they had caught in the act of adultery? That's what our text today tells us. What could have prompted such action? Perhaps it was the result of some scheming in an earlier conversation that went somewhat like this: "There must be some way to get at Him," Elias was saying to the group huddled closely in the corner of the inn. "Perhaps some violation of Roman law that He doesn't know about."

"I'm not sure we should get the Romans involved just yet," responded Ahab, the Pharisee.

"But what then?" inquired Amos, almost in desperation. "We've got to discredit Him or prosecute Him or do something to stop His popularity among the masses."

Finally shrewd Jonathan spoke: "I've been thinking about our own laws of Moses. Jesus of Nazareth claims to fulfill the Law even though He has His own interpretation of it. Why don't we confront Him with a law that is ambiguous enough so that whichever way He answers He loses."

"That sounds great," Ahab responded. "But what law? Others have tried, you know, and Jesus always comes out the winner."

Jonathan was undisturbed. "I've been working on this for some time. I suggest we use the law concerning the stoning of an adulteress. If Jesus says she should not be stoned, we can say He is clearly preaching contrary to the law of Moses. If He says she should be stoned, He will be opposing the Sanhedrin, because they do not enforce this law, and He will also be in opposition to the Romans, because they reserve the death penalty for themselves and would never condemn an adulteress to death."

"You're correct on that point at least," Elias chimed in. "The Romans would prefer to honor an adulteress with a long life."

"It sounds good to me." Amos was thinking now. "In fact we could make it quite dramatic if we take a woman whom we had caught in the act of adultery and presented her to Jesus for a decision, to stone or not to stone."

"But how are we going to catch a woman committing adultery?" Ahab wanted to know. Turning to Elias he added: "Unless you can arrange that with some of the shady characters you know."

"I just think I might be able to do that. Give me a little time. You'll get a real eyeful! Should I also check on the law from Moses so that we are precise in our quotations?"

"I've already done that," Jonathan explained. "Here they are: Leviticus 20:10 talks of the man who commits adultery with another man's wife and concludes: 'The adulterer and the adulteress shall surely be put to death.' By the way, Elias, we don't want the man. Let him get away."

"I was counting on that, Jonathan. You see, the arranger will have to be the seducer for the sum of money we pay him."

"The other main passages are from Deuteronomy 22. First, it again speaks of a man committing adultery with a married woman. It says: 'both of them shall die.' Then the chapter talks about a virgin who is betrothed and another man commits adultery with her. It says, and again I quote: 'You shall stone them with stones that they die.' "

"That should be enough for us," Ahab concluded. "Now it's up to you, Elias, to arrange it and let us know the time."

So it was according to the story recorded in John 8:1-11, that a group of Scribes and Pharisees brought to Jesus one morning, as He taught in the temple, a woman caught in the act of adultery.

(The story is in fine print in the Revised Standard Version of the Bible and in brackets in *Good News for Modern Man*. It seems it was not a part of the original Gospel that John wrote but was inserted from the oral tradition or some early document. In any case it can well be a true incident even if it is not a part of John's writing.)

### Dealing with the Stony Heart

How did our Lord react? How did He escape their intrigue? Our text relates:

"Jesus bent down and wrote with His finger on the ground. and as they continued to ask Him, He stood up and said to them, 'Let him who is without sin among you be the first to throw a stone at her.' And once more He bent down and wrote with His finger on the ground. But when they heard it, they went away, one by one, beginning with the eldest, and Jesus was left alone with the woman standing before Him."

Now what would He do? He was without sin. Should He throw stones? She was certainly guilty. She had been caught in the act. There were eyewitnesses. She did not deny it. She was guilty. She had broken the law. But instead of real stones, or even figurative stones of condemnation, scolding or rebuke, Jesus throws stones of acceptance, love, and forgiveness.

"Jesus looked up and said to her, 'Woman, where are they? Has no one condemned you?' She said, 'No one, Lord.' And Jesus said, 'Neither do I condemn you; go, and do not sin again.' "

Think about the contrasting attitudes. The Scribes and the Pharisees treat this woman as an object to fulfill their purposes. They are eager to condemn and punish for breaking the law. The opposite spirit, which Jesus displays, is one of acceptance and forgiveness. Now try to find situations in which either of these attitudes is present today. Make some modern comparisons or applications. I'll suggest a few starters, but then you keep thinking of your own experience and your own life, of times and places where we figuratively throw stones of condemnation and judgment or of acceptance and forgiveness.

Obviously one comparison would be the girl who "gets into trouble" in our family, in our congregation or community. An unmarried woman has an abortion or a baby. How is she treated? How do you treat her? More like the villains in the story? Or more like Jesus?

Other starters: A young man is caught with a gang in a pot party. A teen-ager is charged with "minor in possession." A wife goes out with another man while her husband is away. A husband gambles away his paycheck. What kind of stones do you throw? Or maybe you try to be completely neutral and are not ready to either condemn or forgive. Something like this:

At a lay evangelism mission in Kansas City one team of callers was enthused over the promise of a man to visit church on Sunday morning. They met him at the door and proudly took the family into the service. After the service they introduced their new friends to the pastor and then tried to get them acquainted with other members of the congregation. I watched and was shocked to see many of the members carefully avoid an introduction or, after being introduced, coolly greet them and walk away. Later I discovered the reason. The man was known in the community as the owner of a bar down the street from the church. The members were not ready to accept as a member of their parish a man who ran a bar. What kind of stones were they throwing? They probably didn't realize it, but they were throwing stones of judgment and rejection. At least, few of them were ready to accept and love.

### Dealing with the Crushed Heart

The first thing that is necessary if I am going to learn to throw stones of forgiveness instead of condemnation is: Let God be the Judge. As Jonathan checked out his passages from the law of Moses on adultery, so I have checked out the passages from the lips of my Lord Jesus Christ and His chief apostle, Paul, on what they say in the New Testament about judgment:

Luke 6:37: "Judge not, and you will not be judged: condemn not, and you will not be condemned; forgive, and you will be forgiven."

Romans 14:10, 12-13: "Why do you pass judgment on your brother? Or you, why do you despise your brother? . . . Each of us shall give account of himself to God. Then let us no more pass judgment on one another but rather decide never to put a stumbling block or hindrance in the way of a brother."

James 4:11-12: "Do not speak evil against one another, brethren. He that speaks evil against a brother or judges his brother speaks evil against the law and judges the law. . . . There is one Lawgiver and Judge, He who is able to save and to destroy. But who are you that you judge your neighbor?"

The first point, then, in getting free from stone throwing is to "let God be the Judge." The second point is to "forgive as God forgives." Jesus did not say to the adulteress, "I'll forgive you if you promise not to do it again." In Luke 7 (36-50) is another story of an adulteress. This one comes voluntarily, washes the feet of Jesus with her tears, wipes them with her hair, and anoints them with oil. Again Jesus exacts no promise but only says, "Your faith has saved you. Go in peace."

Our human nature, which operates by what we call "law," wants to insist: "Get some promise, get a guarantee, get some kind of assurance before you accept or forgive. They'll do the same thing again, and you turn out to be a naive fool."

That's precisely the marvel of God's forgiveness: it's free, complete, absolute—with no conditions. He says: "It is the gift of God—not because of works" (Eph. 2:8-9). "Come, . . . and I will give" (Matt. 11:28). When I come, God accepts me, forgives me, and puts His Spirit within. He does this because of His love and grace in which His own Son Jesus Christ died and rose as my Substitute, in payment for my sin. Now the Spirit of God leads my life and struggles with the evil nature that is "me," that is still weak and still fails. And when I fail, God accepts again and forgives again and again and again.

But I am able to grow, to mature, to overcome sin because of God's Spirit. I can learn to love, as St. Paul says in 1 Corinthians 13, with the kind of love that is "patient and kind," that "bears all things, believes all things, hopes all things, endures all things." This growth can come only when I have been freed from sin, because the growth is produced by the Spirit of God rather than by any human coercion. This is living under God's forgiveness. It is living under the Gospel.

Having experienced this kind of forgiveness, I can forgive others in the same way. In visiting "Teen Challenge" in New York, where David Wilkerson, of *The Cross and the Switchblade* fame, has his center in working with those who have problems with drugs, I heard three people tell their stories. One was a 38-year-old black who had been on drugs for 20 years and had maintained his expensive habit by stealing and picking pockets. The second was an 18-year-old Puerto Rican who had used drugs since he was 14 and had pushed drugs through high school. The third was a brilliant college student whose father was a wealthy businessman. As they each told of their experiences in struggling with the use of drugs and in kicking the habit, one message kept coming through: "We are free! No more slaves to the stuff. We have a new life. We are free to live, to grow in this life. We can use it for God in our own way." That's what this is all about: throwing forgiveness instead of stones. When we come to Christ like this woman, we are set free. We go in peace and sin no more. We can say the same to those around us. We don't have to judge and condemn. We don't have to force reform and make laws for new life. We leave that to God. We accept people, love them, forgive them, trust them, and when they fail, we forgive again—up to seventy times seven.

It's risky? Is God's forgiveness to you risky?

Let the Spirit of God take control, and you are ready to risk for Him.

(Sermon revised from the 1972 *Concordia Pulpit*)

### Parallel Scripture Readings

Luke 7:36-50   Luke 6:37-42 Romans 12:14-21   Matthew 18:21-22

### Suggested Hymns

Jesus Sinners Doth Receive
Lord Jesus Think on Me
My Hope is Built on Nothing Less
May We Thy Precepts Lord Fulfill

# WOMEN OF THE BIBLE

*Hannah*

## My Aim in Life

I SAMUEL 1:10-11, 19-28; 2:19-21

(This sermon is designed to allow for specific involvement of the congregation. A small sheet of paper can be distributed beforehand with the three statements and brief outline shown below, allowing room for hearers to write their response at the points indicated in the sermon.

With minor adaptations the sermon can be used without such specific involvement of the congregation.)

### MY AIM IN LIFE

1. MY AIM IN LIFE IS: _____

_____

2. HANNAH'S AIM IN LIFE WAS: _____

_____

1. She was a loving wife.
2. She carried a heavy cross.
3. She had a devout faith.
4. She was a devoted mother.

3. MY AIM IN LIFE WILL BE: _____

_____

Evaluate: Whom do I seek to please?
1. Self?
2. Others?
3. Self?

How do I choose?
1. I remember who I am.
2. I receive strength from Christ.
3. I commit myself.

There is a parable of life in the story of the farmer whose dog followed him to town one day. As he hitched his horse and buggy to a post in front of the country store, the storekeeper, seeing the panting dog, chided the farmer for making the dog run all the way while he rode. The farmer responded, "That dog is not tired from following me to town. What tired him was all his foolish zigzagging. There was not an open gate, a hole in the fence, or a tree stump that he did not explore. He is tired from all his zigzagging."

That's the way many people live. They zigzag from one diversion to another, from one pleasure to another, from one excitement to another. They wear themselves out but really don't know where they are going. They just chase everything that appears. Robert Burns, the famous poet, confessed late in life, "The misfortune of my life was want of an aim."

Does your life suffer from "want of an aim"? Do you know where you're going, whom you are following? What is your real purpose? Have you ever put it into words? Most of us, I suspect, have never talked to anyone about it or ever written it out. But this morning try to write down what you feel at this moment is your aim. Fill in the first of the three statements on your card. No one else needs to see what you write—just you and God. And after you finish all three statements, you can take the card home and think about it this week.

We will review the life of Hannah, who was a woman with an aim. That will help us fill in the second statement. Then, as the Holy Spirit works on our hearts, let's see at the end of the sermon today whether He has led any of us to make any change in our aim, if we want to write anything different for No. 3: "MY AIM IN LIFE *WILL BE*"than what we write in No. 1: "MY AIM IN LIFE IS."

## I. What Was the Aim of Hannah?
### She Was a Loving Wife

The story of Hannah is recorded in First Samuel 1 and 2. I will summarize her life in four statements, but I hope you read the full account at home this week.

Hannah lived in a small town, Ramah, in the hill country of Ephraim. Ramah was probably some fifteen miles west of Shiloh and about twenty miles northwest of Jerusalem. Hannah lived there with her husband Elkanah, another wife, Peninnah, and the children of Peninnah. It was common in the Old Testament, as you know, for a man to have two wives, especially if there was some circumstance that led up to it, as Jacob with Leah and Rachel, Abraham with Sarah and Hagar. Perhaps Elkanah had married Hannah out of love, but since she was childless, he married Peninnah to bear children and thus escape the disgrace of having no children and losing his family heritage. The short account in First Samuel doesn't explain all this, but it does indicate clearly that Elkanah loved his wife Hannah. When he was sad because she was childless, he comforted her, saying, "Am I not better than ten sons?"

Each year Elkanah would take his family to the tabernacle at Shiloh for the fulfilling of a family vow. A part of the sacrificed animal was eaten by the family in a special ceremonial meal. When Elkanah divided the meat, he always gave a special portion to Hannah, for, as the text explains, "he loved Hannah." There is no reason to question that this love was mutual. So we think of Hannah and Elkanah as a couple living in a deep love relationship.

### She Carried a Heavy Cross

But Hannah was childless, and this was considered a disgrace. It was believed that children were the direct blessing of God; and when a woman had no children, it was said, as in our text: "The Lord had shut up her womb." Peninnah may not have had the love of Elkanah to the same extent that Hannah did, but she did have children. And she let Hannah know about it. Verse six says: "Her adversary provoked her." The Hebrew word for adversary means "rival" and comes from a root word that means "vex" and was used only for a fellow wife.

Hannah felt deeply this shortcoming in her life. She failed her husband. She was inadequate. So it was that in this indicent in First Samuel she leaves the family meal because of the ridicule of Penninnah. She weeps and grieves and in bitterness of soul begs the Lord to take away this heavy cross.

### She Had a Devout Faith

When Hannah prayed, it was more than a pious wish. She was praying to her Lord, who had power to give her children. The term "Lord of hosts" is used in this text for the first time in the Bible. The "hosts" refer to the armies of Israel. He was the Lord who had called Abraham and blesed Isaac and Jacob, the Lord who led the people of Israel to the Promised Land. The psalmist in Psalm 130 says: "Out of the depths have I cried unto You." So Hannah out of her misery was reaching out for help from the only One who could help, the Lord of hosts.

Eli saw her anguished prayer, her lips moving as the words were spoken deep in her spirit, but he thought she was drunk. When he learned otherwise, he wished her peace and grace. Almost as if this were already her answer, Hannah went back to her family "no more sad." God had indeed heard, and we read: "The Lord remembered her, and in due time Hannah conceived and bore a son." Now she could say again with the psalmist: "I called upon the Lord, and He heard my voice." When Samuel was born, she said, "I have asked him of the Lord," like many Old Testament people before her. Eve said, "I have gotten a man from the Lord" (Gen. 4:1). Jacob, when he met his brother Esau after his exile, pointed to his many children and said, "The children which God has graciously given me" (Gen. 33:5). The psalmist sings: "Children are an heritage of the Lord; and the fruit of the womb is His reward" (Ps. 127:3). God not only gave her one son in Samuel but later three more sons and two daughters.

### She Was a Devoted Mother

Hannah was quite a woman—a loving wife with a heavy cross but a devout faith; and then we must add that she was a devoted mother. After Samuel was born and it came time for the annual pilgrimage to Shiloh, which must have had some of the aspects of a family vacation, she decided to give this up because it wouldn't be good for her baby to make the trip. She reported to Elkanah that she was going to omit the trip until her baby was weaned, was finished nursing, which in those days would be two or three years. Elkanah respected her judgment as a mother and said, "Do what seemeth thee good . . . only the Lord establish His Word." It was like saying: "You know best. Let God's will be done." When Samuel was weaned, Hannah made a great ceremony—with an offering of a bull and a bottle of wine—in presenting her child to the Lord, to live in the tabernacle, to serve as a full-time minister under the tutorage of priest Eli. Now she would see her son only once a year on the yearly trip, and then she would bring him a new change of clothes that she had lovingly made during the year.

Yes, a devoted mother, one who thought of her child not as her own to do with as she pleased, not to give satisfaction and pleasure to her, but to do as the Lord pleased. A school superintendent was one night speaking to a parent-teacher meeting. The business meeting was long, so it was late by the time he got to speak. As he looked over the drowsy crowd, he knew he had to do something dramatic to get their full attention. Looking around, he saw a mother holding a sleeping child in the front row. "How much would you take for your child?" The mother hesitated. "Mister, I would not sell him for a million dollars. But you may hold him awhile." Our children belong to God. We hold them awhile for Him. We provide for them, love them, train them, equip them so that one day they stand on their own feet and live their own lives for the Lord. That was Hannah. Now what do you think was her aim in life? Write it down as your second statement. You may have different aims—and different than the one I wrote down, which I'll tell you later.

## II. My Aim in Life

Now we move to the hardest part of your work this morning, thinking through your aim in life and trying to evaluate it. One way to check your aim is examine the target. I can aim at either of three major targets: myself, other people, or God.

Most people aim at themselves. They live to please themselves, to satisfy their own desires to accumulate what they want and what brings pleasure to them at the moment. A New York telephone company analyzed 500 telephone conversations and discovered that the most frequently used word was "I." It was used more then 4,000 times in those 500 short conversations. By nature we are all this way; we put "I" at the center; what we do is determined by what "I" want.

Some people aim at pleasing others, and that becomes their goal in life. You may have put down as your aim or as Hannah's: to serve others, to serve her children, to please her husband. God made us family style, and for each of us our spouse and children do and should play a big role in our lives. But when we talk about our *Aim in Life,* we are talking about the overriding determining factor. If it is children, we are in trouble, for children grow up and leave; if it is spouse, we are in trouble, for spouses die or leave. It may be that our calling is to live a single life—so we have no spouse or children to please.

It is also possible to aim at pleasing other people because we want their approval, we want them to accept us and say nice things about us; so we go along with the crowd and do what we think pleases them. This can be extremely dangerous to our own personality and Christian character. We become so concerned with what other people expect and think that we cannot be ourselves and are afraid to take a stand for what we believe.

I can aim at pleasing myself, pleasing other people, or pleasing God. The big overall aim is to love and please God. This is what I put down as Hannah's aim: to please God. She loved her husband, she served her children, because this is the way she was pleasing God. She gave her son Samuel to the Lord to please God. Her motive was love and gratitude. The first and great commandment of Scripture is: "Thou shalt love the Lord thy God with all thy heart and with all thy soul and with all thy mind."

How do I choose my aim? I may want to choose the kind of aim that Hannah had but not be capable of making that kind of decision. I may have some pet sins I don't want to give up. I may be afraid of what will happen to me. When we live to please God, we may be ridiculed by our own friends and family. When Robert Short, author of *The Gospel According to Peanuts* and *Parables of Peanuts,* spoke at Concordia Teachers College in Seward, he told how as a high school student in Midland, Texas, he became an agnostic although raised in a Methodist home. He became president of the science club, whose activity caused such a stir that the high school principal complained to his parents. He related sitting across the table from his mother as she spoke to him. Tears were running down her cheeks as she said, "I thought we raised you right. I never thought it would come to this: our son an agnostic." During his college years Robert Short, through contacts with a campus pastor, found a new relationship to Jesus Christ and decided to become a minister. He went home to tell his mother about his decision. They were sitting at the same table. Again tears rolled down her cheeks as she said, "I never thought it would come to this: my son a religious fanatic." When you commit your life to God, when you live to please Him, you might be considered a religious fanatic by your own family or friends. There are times when to please God you may displease others or you may even have to deny yourself. So I or others cannot serve as the complete aim of my life.

I cannot make this decision by my own will. It must be an act prompted by the Spirit of God, and that Spirit works as I remember the grace and love of God in Jesus Christ. I remember who I am. Everyone of us can say, "I am a person God loved so much He sent His only son to die for me. I am a Christian, not because I chose to be but as Jesus said: 'You have not chosen Me; I have chosen you.' It was in my baptism that God came into my life and laid His claim upon me. I was buried with Christ. My sinful nature died. I rose a new person, and I can say with Paul, 'It is no longer I that live but Christ that liveth in me.' " Luther once said, "If someone were to knock on the door of my heart and ask who lived here, I would say, 'Martin Luther used to live here, but he has moved out, and Jesus Christ has moved in.' " That's why I am called a Christian—a little Christ. So to make a commitment about my aim in life, I must receive the strength to do it from the Christ that lives in me. In 1 Corinthians Paul talks about eating supernatural food and drinking supernatural drink, which is Christ. In His Word and in His sacrament I receive the vitamins that give me spiritual nourishment so that I can run the race, I can fight the fight, I can work in the vineyard.

And this is a commitment that I make under the control of the Spirit of Christ living in me. I want to put down on my sheet this morning: "My aim in life will be to please God." How about you? Instead of zigzagging through this week, will you say to your Lord that in all your relationships to others, to your spouse, your children, in your work, in your leisure you will try to live and act in a way that pleases God?

It is said that Dick Van Dyke once had a motto on his desk: "I'm No. 3." When asked about it he would explain: "God is first; others are second; I am third." Write down your aim as your personal commitment to make God first.

(Revised sermon from the 1972 *Concordia Pulpit*)

### Parallel Scripture Readings

Philippians 3:12-16     Matthew 22:34-40  John 12:20-26  Luke 24:23-27

### Suggested Hymns

I Gave My Life for Thee
Thee Will I Love, My Strength, My Tower
Oh, Blest the House
Awake My Soul and with the Sun

# WOMEN OF THE BIBLE

*Mary and Martha*

## Doing Our Own Thing

LUKE 10:38-42; JOHN 11:5, 20-27, 32; 12:1-3

This is an age of self-expression and of freeing up self to be oneself. The desire of people today is to be whole persons and to lead self-fulfilling lives.

"I want to be free—I've got to be me," we used to sing in a song of the day. "To each his own" is another way of putting it. "I've got to do my thing" is a common expression.

Such statements could be expressions of a very self-centered, selfish way of living. On the other hand, they could also be genuinely indicative of honest desire to be what God intended us to be, and sincere verbal attempts to achieve a goal of self-fulfillment, of being real people in relation to God, self, and fellowmen.

The Biblical accounts of the two well-known sisters, Mary and Martha, have been used to prove many things: lessons in hospitality; devotion to Jesus; achieving life's highest goal and good, that of sitting at Jesus' feet hearing His Word; doing "the one thing needful." All these are in these accounts, to be sure. But these episodes from the lives of Mary and Martha also exemplify the matter of

### Doing Our Own Thing
#### Mary and Martha Each Did Her Own Thing

Three episodes from the lives of Mary and Martha appear in Scripture, excerpts of which comprise our text. One doesn't have to read them with much concentration to realize that here are two very different persons; though sisters, each one displayed certain patterns of personality and performance.

Watch for the consistent characteristics of each as we briefly review the three accounts. Mary invariably ended up at Jesus' feet, did a lot of listening, and rarely said anything; Martha was always busily bustling about preparing and serving food to guests or running out to Jesus, impulsively telling Him something that was on her mind.

**Episode One:**
**Martha Serves and Complains: Mary Sits and Listens**

In the first episode Martha seemingly was the perfect hostess. Jesus had come to the village of Bethany, where Martha immediately welcomed Jesus into her house. Having done so, she busied herself with much serving while her sister Mary sat quietly at Jesus' feet listening to His teaching. This bothered Martha, so she barged in where the two of them were and blurted out, "Lord, don't You care that my sister has left me alone to serve? Tell her then to help me." Martha serves and speaks her mind. Mary is content to listen to what Jesus has to say; and she does not lash back at her sister, so far as we know.

**Episode Two:**
**Martha Runs and Talks: Mary Sits and Thinks**

The second episode: Lazarus, the brother of Mary and Martha, has become ill and died. Though the sisters had sent for Jesus during the illness, Jesus had delayed His coming. Finally, after Lazarus had been dead four days, Jesus comes. Wouldn't you know it? Martha rushes out to meet Jesus and once again blurts out in her outspoken way, "Lord, if You had been here, my brother would not have died." There is a ring of faith in her words, however, especially as she goes on to say, "Even now I know that whatsoever You ask from God, God will give You." All this is climaxed with a beautiful statement of faith: "I believe, Lord, that You are the Christ, the Son of God, He who is coming into the world."

Where is Mary during all this? While Martha goes out to meet Jesus, Mary sits in the house, quietly grieving. Thereafter, when Martha calls Mary and tells her that Jesus is calling for her, Mary quickly leaves the house to find Jesus. When she comes to Him, typically she falls at His feet and says about the same words as her sister had spoken. Even in crisis and grief Martha and Mary did their own thing, following their predictable patterns of behavior.

**Episode Three:**
**Martha Serves: Mary Quietly Sacrifices**

Now the third report about the sisters and Jesus. It was six days before the Passover. A supper was prepared for Jesus in the house of Simon the leper. Lo and behold, who should be serving again but Martha? Suddenly Mary is at Jesus' feet again, this time anointing Him with a very costly, fragrant ointment, wiping His feet with her hair. Again we see each of the sisters doing her own thing.

### Whose Performance Was Better?

Who do you think was more right than the other in doing her thing—Mary or Martha? Mary, it seems, was a contemplative person; Martha was an activist. Mary was a good listener, Martha a willing servant. Mary was absorbed in the theoretical; Martha was engaged in the practical. Mary spent her money on perfume to anoint Jesus; Martha purchased and prepared food and served Jesus. Mary is often set up by the casual Bible reader as the ideal Christian person; Martha often comes out as the heel.

### Jesus Loved Both; He Condemned Neither

Whose performance was more acceptable? The answer is in a statement the evangelist John makes: "Now Jesus loved Martha and her sister." So He loved them both—Mary as the one who always sat at His feet, Martha as the impetuous, impulsive one who always served and said what she thought. Yet Mary is the criticized one. Her sister, Martha, castigated her because she just sat there and wouldn't help with the serving: "Lord, don't You care that my sister has left me to serve alone? Tell her then to help me." When you get right down to it, Martha was criticizing Jesus, the Son of God, in what she said. Later Mary was criticized by Judas because she wasted all that good perfume on Jesus' feet when it might have been sold and the proceeds given to the poor. In each instance Jesus rose to the defense of Mary, as first He told Martha: "Mary has chosen the good portion, which shall not be taken away from her." In speaking to Judas and to others who were criticizing Mary's extravagance, He said: "Let her alone; why do you trouble her? She has done a beautiful thing to Me. For you always have the poor with you, and whenever you will, you can do good to them; but you will not always have Me. She has done what she could" Jesus defended and commended Mary for doing her thing.

As for Martha, nowhere did Jesus actually condemn her activistic conduct. It was only when she became critical of her sister's actions or lack of action, her attempt to do her thing, that Jesus gently rebuked Martha with the words: "Martha, Martha, you are anxious and troubled about many things; one thing is needful. Mary has chosen the good portion."

### Jesus Loves, Rebukes, Forgives

Actually it's rather difficult to determine which of these two women Jesus loved more and whose conduct He approved of most. Probably the one as much as the other. Where they failed—Mary in her lack of action for Him and Martha in her sometimes hyperactivity—He forgave them. He loved them both with all their faults, whatever they were, as they were spontaneously lost in doing their thing for Him.

Who, then, in life is right—more right than another—in doing his own thing? Listening to the voice of God and never doing anything for Him can be as useless as always doing without listening to God's Word for guidance and direction. The one might be laziness and lethargy; the other, useless activism and even fanaticism. Martha could have used some of the simple, quiet faith Mary had; and undoubtedly Mary could have learned from her sister to be a little more expressive of her faith and active for the Lord— which she finally became and did when she anointed the Savior's feet in the last episode. Doing one's thing "no matter what" can in fact be very selfish, misguided, wrong, and harmful, as demonstrated by some of today's anarchistic political philosophies, chronic dissatisfaction, irresponsible living, unreasonable demanding, opportunity seeking, greed, rioting, and war. But if we're really doing our thing as redeemed, forgiven children of our heavenly Father, out of love for our Savior, who loves and gave Himself for us, growing in His grace and serving Him, listening attentively to His Word and will, then if we make mistakes or go off the deep end, we know that He will correct us and forgive us and give us another chance. But we ought to be careful about criticizing others who are earnestly doing their thing for Him, remembering that He loves them as well as us.

## The Most Right Thing to Do

All this brings us to the grand climax of the Mary-Martha episodes in Scripture: that there is practical, lasting, eternal value in doing whatever we do with guidance from the Word of God. "This," says Jesus, is still "the one thing needful . . . the good portion which shall not be taken away." This is the basic and most right thing to do.

Accordingly we can do our thing best if we start by doing the best thing first: not losing our heads in the clouds of our own imagination or idealism nor yet burying our heads in the humanistic dust of our own good deeds but getting down to the feet of Jesus, opening our eyes and perking up our ears to see and hear the will and Word of God. That's where the beginning of action is.

### Here We Find the Answers

There at the feet of Jesus we find answers to such important personal, perplexing questions as: Who am I? Why do I make such dreadful mistakes of judgment and miscalculation? Why do I live and serve so meaninglessly and blindly? Why do I hurt people so often and offend God so much? Why is my tongue so sharp and critical, my heart so stubborn, my mind so often filled with evil thoughts and desires, my desired self-sufficiency so insufficient, my judgment so poor, my strength so weak, my temper so terrible, my jealousy so green? If I listen, I hear the voice of God telling me: "My son, my daughter, the imagination of man's heart is evil from his youth." And again: "There is not a just man upon earth who does good and never sins." But Jesus goes on to say: "Though it is true that the soul who sins shall die, because the wages of sin is death; nonetheless the gift of God is eternal life. Believe in Me. Your faith has saved you. Go and sin no more. Go and serve with gladness. Go and do your thing."

There at Jesus' feet we learn that we are going to be criticized for our faith and its expression. When Martha came running to Jesus all upset about Mary just sitting there listening to the voice of her God, Jesus didn't condemn the Martha He loved but simply called her to order: "Martha, Martha, you are anxious and troubled about many things; but Mary has chosen the one thing needful, which shall not be taken away from her." Jesus did not condemn Martha for doing her activist thing, but He did criticize her for criticizing another who was doing her thing in her own way.

### Jesus Does Not Try to Change Personalities

Jesus never did try to change the personalities of Martha and Mary, though He did condemn the wrong and approve the right. The one continued to be an activist; the other remained a reflective and contemplative person. The one went right on busying herself serving; the other preferred her life-style at Jesus' feet. Yet they both got the message. Both end up serving: the one serving at tables; the other anointing Jesus' feet, probably always preoccupied with doing the more beautiful, esthetic things in life.

### Doing the Best Thing in Crisis

But when a crisis came, when Lazarus, their brother, died, both Mary and Martha not only did their own thing, they did the best thing as both sought counsel at Jesus' feet. True to her nature, Martha came running to Jesus first with a somewhat caustic remark: "Lord, if You had been here, my brother would not have died." But there was faith in Jesus behind those words; there was a sincere searching for an answer to her grief and perplexity. She was not just looking for an answer but possibly, in faith, also looking for a miracle. Jesus replied to her with some of the most beautiful words recorded in Scripture: "I am the Resurrection and the Life;

he who believes in Me, though he were dead, yet shall he live; and he who lives and believes in Me shall never die. Do you believe this?" When Mary at length also came running to Jesus for answers, Jesus gave her even more than words: He performed the miracle of raising Lazarus from the dead. The thing called faith was not in vain.

So we too go on in life, each of us doing our own thing. That's how our Lord made us, and that's what He expects of us, knowing full well that we will fall and fail again and again. He wants us to do our thing, to use our unique talents and personalities. But in and through it all He wants us always to be aware of "the thing" He did for us when He gave His life that we might do our thing. It is His natural expectation of us that we come running to Him day after day, hearing His Word, faithfully doing "the one thing needful." As we do, He gives us the cleansing we need, the answers of life we seek, and the power and motivation to do our thing all our days, in love to Him and in service to our fellowmen.

(Revised Sermon from the 1972 *Concordia Pulpit)*

### Parallel Scripture Readings

Colossians 1:21-28     Ephesians 4:1-11     1 Corinthians 12:1-11

### Suggested Hymns

One Thing's Needful; Lord, This Treasure
Thee Will I Love, My Strength, My Tower
Take My Life and Let It Be